ASTROLOGY

ASTROLOGY
YOUR GUIDE TO THE STARS

TOPHI BOOKS

Unit 5A, 202–208 New North Road,
London N1 7BJ, England

Contents

The Signs of the Zodiac and How to Interpret Them 1

THE SIGNS LISTED—THE ASTROLOGICAL CALENDAR—
TWELVE TYPES OF HUMANITY—ANCIENT AND MODERN
INTERPRETATIONS—BASIC POINTS OF ASTROLOGY

The Sign of Aries: The Ram 9

BIRTH DATES MARCH 21–APRIL 19

ARIES CALENDAR—SYMBOLS—ACTION—ADVAN-
TAGES—REQUIREMENTS—VARIATIONS—EARLY AND
LATE PERIODS

The Sign of Taurus: The Bull 21

BIRTH DATES APRIL 19–MAY 20

TAURUS CALENDAR—SYMBOLS—TYPICAL TRAITS—CON-
STRUCTIVE QUALITIES—REQUIREMENTS—VARIATIONS—
EARLY AND LATE PERIODS

The Sign of Gemini: The Twins 33

BIRTH DATES MAY 20–JUNE 21

GEMINI CALENDAR—SYMBOLS—A QUICK NATURE—EX-
TREMES OF GEMINI—REQUIREMENTS—VARIATIONS—
EARLY AND LATE PERIODS

The Sign of Cancer: The Crab 45

BIRTH DATES JUNE 21–JULY 22

CANCER CALENDAR—SYMBOLS—A SIGN OF SUCCESS—
SPECIAL EXAMPLES—REQUIREMENTS—VARIATIONS—
EARLY AND LATE PERIODS

The Sign of Leo: The Lion 57

BIRTH DATES JULY 22–AUGUST 22

LEO CALENDAR—SYMBOLS—ATTAINMENT OF AMBI-
TION—DEVELOPMENT OF LEO NATURE—REQUIRE-
MENTS—VARIATIONS—EARLY AND LATE PERIODS

The Sign of Virgo: The Virgin 69

BIRTH DATES AUGUST 22–SEPTEMBER 23

VIRGO CALENDAR—SYMBOLS—AN ADAPTIVE MEN-
TALITY—VAGARIES OF VIRGO—REQUIREMENTS—VARIA-
TIONS—EARLY AND LATE PERIODS

The Sign of Libra: The Scales 81

BIRTH DATES SEPTEMBER 23–OCTOBER 23

LIBRA CALENDAR—SYMBOLS—THE SIGN OF INTUITION—
WELL-WEIGHED FACTORS—REQUIREMENTS—VARIA-
TIONS—EARLY AND LATE PERIODS

The Sign of Scorpio: The Scorpion 93

BIRTH DATES OCTOBER 23–NOVEMBER 21

SCORPIO CALENDAR—SYMBOLS—A SIGN OF SELF-CON-
TROL—A SECRETIVE NATURE—REQUIREMENTS—VARIA-
TIONS—EARLY AND LATE PERIODS

The Sign of Sagittarius: The Bowman 105

BIRTH DATES NOVEMBER 22–DECEMBER 21

SAGITTARIUS CALENDAR—SYMBOLS—SETTING A STAN-
DARD—HONESTY AND CONFIDENCE—REQUIREMENTS—
VARIATIONS—EARLY AND LATE PERIODS

The Sign of Capricorn: The Goat 117

BIRTH DATES DECEMBER 21–JANUARY 20

CAPRICORN CALENDAR—SYMBOLS—THE NEED FOR CON-
FIDENCE—AN ABIDING NATURE—REQUIREMENTS—VARI-
ATIONS—EARLY AND LATE PERIODS

The Sign of Aquarius: The Water Carrier 129

BIRTH DATES JANUARY 20–FEBRUARY 19

AQUARIUS CALENDAR—AN APTITUDE FOR ACHIEVE-
MENT—ACCEPTANCE OF ADVICE—REQUIREMENTS—
VARIATIONS—EARLY AND LATE PERIODS

The Sign of Pisces: The Fishes 141

BIRTH DATES FEBRUARY 19–MARCH 21

PISCES CALENDAR—SYMBOLS—POTENTIAL GREATNESS—
PROTECTION VS. PROCRASTINATION—REQUIREMENTS—
VARIATIONS—EARLY AND LATE PERIODS

The Planets and Their Powers 155

THE PLANETS LISTED—GOVERNING PLANETS—THEIR
IMPORTANCE—PLANETS AND BIRTH SIGNS—VARIANCE
AND INTERMINGLING—CASTING A HOROSCOPE

The Sun 161

The Moon 167

The Planet Mars 173

The Planet Mercury 179

The Planet Jupiter 185

The Planet Venus 193

The Planet Saturn 201

Summary of Planetary Influences 207

Noted Persons Born Under Different Signs 211

EXAMPLES OF BIRTH DATES THROUGH THE ENTIRE
ASTROLOGICAL CALENDAR

History of Astrology 223

Astrology and Your Career 247

Astrological Guide to Decorating 257

Astrology & Diets 267

The Signs of
the Zodiac
and How to
Interpret
Them

From time immemorial, the stars have been regarded as significant in the affairs of men and nations. Even today, the Pole Star guides navigators northward and the handle of the Big Dipper serves as an unerring clock. Below the equator, the Southern Cross is a dominating sight in the night sky. Other constellations, such as Orion, the mighty Hunter, have impressed generations of viewers and have roused the imagination of many keen minds.

But in the lore and tradition of Astrology, the constellations forming the Signs of the Zodiac are of prime significance. There are twelve of these and they are arranged like a crude belt across the sky, completely girdling the earth. Month by month, the Sun moves into a new Sign, so that the Astrological calendar runs about as follows:

ARIES — The Ram — March 21 to April 19
TAURUS — The Bull — April 19 to May 20
GEMINI — The Twins — May 20 to June 21
CANCER — The Crab — June 21 to July 22
LEO — The Lion — July 22 to August 22
VIRGO — The Virgin — August 22 to September 23

LIBRA — The Scales — September 23 to October 23

SCORPIO — The Scorpion — October 23 to November 22

SAGITTARIUS — The Bowman — November 22 to December 21

CAPRICORN — The Goat — December 21 to January 20

AQUARIUS — The Water Carrier — January 20 to February 19

PISCES — The Fishes — February 19 to March 21

Now, each of these Signs is representative of a different type of individual, as will be specified separately in the pages that follow. Our modern calendar does not conform to the ancient Astrological months, so allowance must be made accordingly. One point should be noted, however:

The influence of each sign carries over about one week into the next, so that all persons born in March, for example, will be influenced to some degree by Pisces. But it must be remembered that the influence actually begins before the start of the modern month, as shown by the Astrological Calendar.

The Signs of the Zodiac should be firmly fixed in mind and accepted as the final authority, or confusion may result. But in studying the Twelve Types of humanity, as represented by those signs, it should be remembered that each blends into the one that follows it. Also, due allowance should be made for individual traits, due to Planetary Influences and various governing factors.

The question has often been raised:

How can all persons be placed in a specified Sign when every individual has his or her own distinctive traits, to a degree where no two people in the world can be said to be precisely alike?

This age-old query has its answer in a modern analogy. Only in comparatively recent times did scientists come to recognize that all finger prints are the mark of the individual. It took the public years to believe that billions of such prints might be compared, yet no two sets found to be indentical in every detail.

Yet one of the great advantages of finger print files lies in the fact that any strange or unidentified set can be matched against those on record! This would seem like one chance in a million, an exhaustive task requiring a whole crew of workers. But no, the job is almost entirely automatic, for one simple reason:

Despite their distinctive differences, all finger prints are formed by whorls, ridges, and varied components that are classified into special groups. These are narrowed, step by step, until finally so few are left that comparison of the few remaining points is easy. But it was only because of the similarity of all prints in certain major groups that this was possible.

Apply the same to Astrology and the Signs of the Zodiac are seen to be the chief classification from which others stem, or may be modified. Only by first placing persons in one of those Twelve Types can their traits be studied in further detail. They are alike that far; beyond that, they are individualistic.

But the basic points, as represented by the Birth Signs, must be strikingly similar, or further classification would be impossible. Thus, two persons born under a Sign like Taurus will have specific traits in common. How many such traits, a study of the Sign will show. But two persons with the same Sign will not be at variance, except where an interpretation of the Sign may indicate that factor.

Some Birth Signs show conflicting natures and it is often possible to analyze many persons in terms of circumstances and companionship, according to the effect that those would logically show in relation to accepted traits. Each Sign is like a background on which the pattern of the individual career is traced, much in the manner of a chart or map.

If you should plan to drive an automobile from New York to Buffalo, a road map would show you various routes, but it would need to be a map of New York State, not one of California. The same applies to the Signs of the Zodiac. Find the right one: Then use it to judge the personal inclinations or life course that it may represent.

In any case, it means making the most of one's own talents; not merely accepting the decree of fate. That is the message summed by Astrology in two potent words:

Know thyself!

♈

The Sign of
ARIES

ARIES THE RAM
(March 21–April 19)

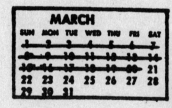

Birth Stone:	Diamond
Birth Flower:	Daisy or Sweet Pea
Harmonious Colors:	Red and Pink
Ruling Planet:	Mars
Best Marriages:	Gemini, Leo, Libra, Sagittarius
	Sometimes with Own Sign: Aries

Action is the word for Aries.

Just as Aries heads the Signs of the Zodiac, so does the letter "A" head the Alphabet. And that "A" sounds a further note, by standing for several other adjectives that are significant of Aries attributes.

Action is what the Aries person craves, because, like the Ram, which is the symbol of his Sign, he not only has force and drive; he is a born leader.

While people with Aries birth dates are eager enough to do things on their own, they usually expect others to follow and intuitively set a pattern that will be attractive to such cohorts.

Let us first appraise some of the assets of Aries, that wonderful Sign that adds the sparkle of a crown jewel to the entire Zodiac. Without Aries as the pace setter, the other Signs would seem very drab, indeed.

For it is Aries that gives us a chance to compare the virtues and vicissitudes represented by those other Signs. It is Aries that "sparks" the entire circuit, to use a term that is both modern and apt.

For Aries is always modern. It is the "Go" signal of the Heavens. Always, the Aries individuals are getting a jump ahead of all the rest, like the name of Abu Ben Adhem.

Here are some of the advantages of Aries, as represented by the always present A.

Advantages of Aries

Being Active, they are Adaptable, always quick to change course or find a new outlet for their remarkable energy, the moment it appears advantageous.

This in turn shows that they are Alert. They are the first to become aware of changed conditions and to conform to newly accepted standards.

As Advisors, they are very Able. Being quick to appraise a situation, they can rouse others of conservative or sluggish natures into action that they would never ordinarily attempt. This is where Aries really sparks things.

All this adds up to Ambition, which the average Aries person considers in the light of Achievement. Those are like the twin horns of the Ram itself.

They can also be the horns of a dilemma, a dubious aspect of the Aries Sign. In their eagerness to show results, persons of this type frequently are satisfied with small ambition and quick achievement.

They will scatter their efforts, dropping one thing and taking up another, whichever looks better at the moment. Not that they dodge obstacles; quite the contrary. Indeed, their tendency to ram away at things often accounts for such sudden shift in purposes.

Requirements of this Sign

Aim is an asset that they need. With all their activity, they generally appear to be heading toward a goal, but it may be a futile one. All that activity makes them Aggressive, an "A" that may or may not be an asset. They also turn Argumentative, which is definitely on the bad side, as when they win an argument, they may mistakenly think that they have proved a point.

These people have been known to do what amounts to a face about, without actually realizing it, provided they sincerely believe that they are fighting for a just cause. They become crusaders and reformers, often bitter in their attacks on persons who offend their accepted standards.

With all this, it may seem surprising that Aries folk, often unable to control themselves, are fitted to advise others. But that is easily explained.

Quick to accept a situation, eager to begin work, fearless when facing issues, they can often stir their hesitant or doubtful friends into action.

Not only that, they provide the spark already mentioned that will energize well formulated plans that some one else has long mulled over. Aries scores one big "A" in providing Answers. They are never at a loss for them.

So others thrive at the expense of Aries, the one Sign which represents a person who may be blindly unable to help himself, though it must be said that many of these persons amble through life with constant and sometimes cumulative success.

But that may be due to their ability to out-argue the opposition, or find new outlets to their advantage. Often luck aids Aries folk, but it must be noted that they are always on the lookout for it.

What to Avoid or Cultivate

Anger is the worst trait of Aries. It is something persons of this Sign should always avoid, as it causes them to cast aside Ambition and resort to Argument, the two things that do not mix.

A big "A" that they need is that of Associations of the right sort; people who will reciprocate in some measure for all that the Aries person offers them. It's hard for Aries people to take on partners; they want to be independent and they hate harness. But they should invite cooperation.

Otherwise, they become bellwethers, the rams that lead the trusting flock to the same old pastures and sometimes to outright ruin. Aries persons are natural Actors and as such they like an Audience, another combination that may be good or bad.

Patience and purpose should be cultivated by persons born under Aries, whose position as Head Men of the Zodiac make them true pioneers, who pave the way for other people to profit. Gaining one's own rightful share should be the Aries aim.

VARIATIONS OF THE ARIES SIGN

The Sign of the Ram is so forceful and quick of action, that less variance is likely to be found among persons with differing birthdays in Aries, than in most other Signs.

The Aries urge, being ever-present, can often outdrive adverse influences. When given its head, it will take the lead. As a result, the Aries temperament is always clearly evidenced by persons born during almost any portion of its period.

The aggressive qualities of Mars, the Ruling Planet, naturally add to all this, so that Aries is sharply defined and strong of influence throughout. But here we find special modifications in:

THE EARLY PERIOD

During the first few days of Aries, this powerful Head Sign utilizes some of the Pisces qualities. The Jupiterian rule over Pisces works well with the Martian forcefulness found in Aries, so that these early birds in the Aries Sign shape up thus:

There is motive to their Aries Activity. They act on hunches, intuitively picking either the best way or some unexpected way to handle an odd situation. They are often regarded as lucky, when it is really a case of them using their heads to guide their feet.

Jupiter tempers the Martian nature, giving these early Rams more influence over people, or a more friendly manner than is found in the generally aggressive Aries person. In all, it is a fine combination.

THE LATE PERIOD

Toward the late portion of the Aries period, the Birth Dates begin to show a marked Taurus trend. Good to a degree, this adds power to the Aries nature. But this can result in too much effort, too much enthusiasm over things that are hardly worth it, or which represent merely one of several issues.

People born late in the Aries calendar may add pile-driver tactics to gain ends which could be attained with only a normal display of energy. They have strong human sympathies of the Venusian class, and these when aroused, will stir the Martian force to feats of derring-do.

The Sign of
TAURUS

TAURUS: THE BULL
(April 19–May 20)

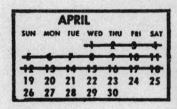

			APRIL			
SUN	MON	TUE	WED	THU	FRI	SAT
			~~1~~	~~2~~	~~3~~	~~4~~
~~5~~	~~6~~	~~7~~	~~8~~	~~9~~	~~10~~	~~11~~
~~12~~	~~13~~	~~14~~	~~15~~	~~16~~	~~17~~	~~18~~
19	20	21	22	23	24	25
26	27	28	29	30		

			MAY			
SUN	MON	TUE	WED	THU	FRI	SAT
					1	2
3	4	5	6	7	8	9
10	11	12	13	14	15	16
17	18	19	~~20~~	~~21~~	~~22~~	~~23~~
~~24~~	~~25~~	~~26~~	~~27~~	~~28~~	~~29~~	~~30~~

Birth Stone:	Emerald or Agate
Birth Flower:	Lily-of-the-Valley or Hawthorn
Harmonious Colors:	Yellow and Blue Red attractive, but inharmonious
Ruling Planet:	Venus
Best Marriages:	Virgo, Libra, Scorpio, Capricorn Other Signs indicate conflict

The letter "B" as the second in the alphabet, appropriately fits the second Sign of the Zodiac, as Taurus, in modern nomenclature, represents a Bull.

That "B" stands for Bravery, Bluntness and Brilliance, while Beauty is often a feminine feature of this Sign.

Critics are quick to define a Taurus person as "bull-headed" and they are very often right. But they may fail to add up all the assets that belong with that implication.

The Sign of the Bull signifies "B" for Brains, as these are the "headiest" of all persons, in every meaning of the term. They know what they want and go after it in the most direct manner, even though it may be the hard way.

Here we find practical, powerful individuals, who gather facts and remember them, being always eager to put such knowledge into use. Some are rather overwhelming in their nature, while others are more staunch and steadfast.

But all are stubborn, as typically so as the Bull which represents their Birth Sign. But that is not to be taken as a bad token, where Taurus is concerned.

These bullish folk often fulfill the adage of being "generous to a fault." On the other hand, they can be "stubborn to a virtue." It's all explained by that urge to have their own way, the hard way.

Typical Taurus Traits

A Taurus type is not content to lead the way. He crashes right through on his own. If others follow, he congratulates them for having helped. Just as often, he will batter down barriers for them.

That is when the Taurus generosity is wasted on persons who do not deserve it. But those who really need whole-hearted help may often gain it from a Taurus person when all other sources have failed, simply because the Taurus type is stubborn enough to fight for a losing cause.

Never goad a Taurus person into anything that he may even think is against his own best interests. If you do, that mad bull may come charging in your direction. You can go along with the Taurus nature, but you can't drive it.

Being strong-willed and self-reliant, persons of this Sign are naturally independent. They are the type who "want what they want when they want it" and they will give way to unbridled passion and outright dissipation if the mood so seizes them.

With them, friendship and conviviality frequently become identical and they adopt the motto, "Eat, drink and be merry" as their one great rule. But when Taurus folk exercise self-control, as they can, there is no telling how high their ambition may rise.

Their only danger then is that they may become intolerant of others, unwilling to excuse the very weaknesses that they have personally conquered. This may be due to a secret fear or even an urge to do the very things that they so roundly condemn. The fact remains: They can be as obstinately set on following the straight and narrow, as they would be toward following the primrose path.

Constructive Qualities

Taurus people are constructive, making good builders, engineers, designers, photographers, succeeding in any field where mental effort takes on a practical aspect. Only when some obstacle confronts them are they likely to show the destructive traits that go with an uncontrolled bullish temperament.

The more powerful they become, the more apt they are to recognize the necessity for restraint. They become devoted to a cause and may serve as a human bulwark. With their bravery goes the surety that they are right.

Remember this: The Signs of the Zodiac are representative of the underlying traits of the individual, not just the outward characteristics. So to liken the Taurus person to a bull does not mean that such an individual must be big, blundering and bombastic. Quite to the contrary:

It is simply that a Taurus person packs power in plenty, regardless of size. When they go "all out" for what they want, or for those they trust, they become diminutive dynamos. But if size, physique and sheer strength are also present in Taurus persons, they will throw all that in for good measure.

That is when they may be rough and ready, particularly if their higher natures are undeveloped. Remember that such persons put everything into the struggle, so if physical prowess is all that they possess, they will make amends for other lacks by using it to the full.

What to Avoid or Cultivate

Thus Taurus persons can be unreasonable to the point where they are downright dangerous. The "T" in Taurus can signify Tantrums, all to be avoided. Mental development is therefore the answer; through it, aggressive qualities can be transmuted into those of endurance, a fine Taurus trait.

By avoiding anger, controlling desire, preferring purity to pleasure, the Taurus person can turn his artistry, brilliance and magnetic qualities into great success, as making money is another ability found in those born under this Sign.

Persistence helps in these things; and those of Taurus have that quality too. You often find them silent as well as self-sufficient, because they have learned that minding their own business brings big dividends.

The more they can do for themselves, the more they can do for others. That about represents the zenith in the development of the Taurus nature.

VARIATIONS OF THE TAURUS SIGN

With the power of anything up to the size of a battleship, persons born under the Sign of the Bull are hard to stop when once in action. Therefore, any underlying influences are mighty important in their natures.

Every Taurus person seems different, even those born to the exact day or hour. This is because even the smallest things to which they are susceptible may become manifest in their greater activities.

This is specially true of those born in:

THE EARLY PERIOD

Ever hear of a "bull in a china shop"? This can be it! The person born early in the Taurus period, even up to the end of the first week may fall right into this class, with all its problems and errors.

Here, the strong Taurus nature, with its sympathy and strength combined, is over-desirous for action, due to the Martian trend that carries over from the **Ram Sign**, which in its turn, is always finding opportunities for a quick, hard drive to an immediate goal.

Thus the early Taurus person, confronted with any unusual or worrisome situation, will try to bull its way out, rather than be content to wait for bigger things.

So such Taurus folk will smash about, breaking chinaware, going skittish whenever a red rag is waved, and in general wasting gigantic energy on dwarfish objectives. They need control, control and more control.

THE LATE PERIOD

Birth dates toward the end of Taurus show the insinuating influence of Gemini, with its Mercurian proclivities. Here the Bull nature is strong as ever, but it begins to show cunning. It makes false passes, draws the opposition off guard and then drives full force to success.

This is by no means good, for such people are not as clever as they think and may blunder badly with their choices. These latter Taurus Birth Dates come under a distinctly Saturnine influence, which throws such persons into gloom when their premature plans fizzle.

♊

The Sign of
GEMINI

GEMINI: THE TWINS
(May 20–June 21)

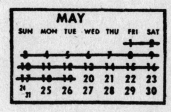

Birth Stone:	Pearl or Beryl Also: Alexandrite
Birth Flower:	Rose or Honeysuckle
Harmonious Colors:	Light Blue and Silvery White
Ruling Planet:	Mercury
Best Marriages:	Aries, Leo, Libra, Aquarius Sometimes with Own Sign: Gemini

This is the Sign of the Twins—represented by the mythological figures of Castor and Pollux—and it symbolizes a dual nature found in persons born under its influence.

Such persons are active, clever, skillful, versatile—and often totally unpredictable. They are always a jump ahead, not only of other people, but sometimes of themselves.

In fact, it has been said of Gemini folk that the one thing you can always expect from them is something unexpected. This is due both to their natural quickness and the twofold aspect of their nature.

Gemini persons are willing to try a hand at almost anything and drop it just as quickly. They pick up things easily, showing such natural talent toward acquiring skills that interest them, that they take it for granted they can learn all there is to know about a subject in very little time.

Whatever they fail at, they dismiss as something not worth bothering about. Thus you find them dropping old projects as fast as they take up new ones.

A Quick Nature

Gemini persons make friends quickly and have a natural ability as salesmen. They are good talkers and come up with new ideas, sometimes borrowing them outright, though they often have plenty of their own.

It is simply that every new thing interests them, rouses their ingenuity and gives them the urge to put it to immediate and profitable use. They go for fads, hobbies and high honors, but often lose interest in them, once they have gained them.

The same applies to their friends. Never being at a loss for new, they neglect the old. But being both clever and practical, they are able to renew old friendships or revive abandoned projects, in that same speedy, breathtaking fashion.

The old saying "Easy come, easy go," often applies to Gemini persons more than those of any other sign. They can make money hand over fist and squander it by literally throwing it away.

There are many born gamblers in the Gemini clan, all the result of these combined factors. They want fast results in the easiest possible way and at the same time are willing to forget a loss and go after a new win.

Extremes of Gemini

From this it can be said that Gemini persons are creatures of the moment, which they are; but that is often a strength more than a weakness. It marks them as great opportunists and in their keen, practical way, they may note something today and make it tomorrow's aim.

Definitely, the Gemini character is that of the extremist. As a result they can be tricky and deceitful; yet at the next moment go overboard in generosity.

All this goes with their active, restless natures. They are great travelers, always eager to be on the go, eager for adventure because their quick thinking makes them masters in emergencies. The modern world is truly made to their order, with its modes of swift travel, need for new inventions and so many varied types of enterprise available.

But such things can lead to Gemini's undoing. People born under this Sign need stability. They can't get it by stacking one thing against another or piling up interests helter-skelter, yet that is the way they usually try.

What to Avoid or Cultivate

In seeking new friends and interests, they yield to the rule "Out of sight, out of mind," as applied to others. The result is, the Gemini person often loses out in business and social affairs, through his own inconstancy and inconsistency.

This causes the Gemini nature to become both skeptical and suspicious. Their very aptitude for picking up where they left off, plus the fact that they have been so busy and active in the meantime, causes them to overlook the damage that neglect can cause.

Gemini's urge to do things differently is another problem. People put up with it, but that doesn't mean they like it or endorse it. Often, a Gemini career becomes one of completely scattered effort and dissipated talents.

By focussing full attention upon worthy projects and carrying them through to completion, Gemini persons can gain great success and at the same time become the most satisfied persons on earth. Quick of wit as well as tact, they have an amazing ability at appraising people as well as situations almost at a glance.

That snap judgment seldom goes wrong in practical matters and the few opportunities they miss are more than compensated by their skilled avoidance of time wasters. They get to the point of things immediately and are always finding short-cuts.

They recognize the importance of appearances and therefore keep up their own. They are good dressers, fond of show, fond of fun, always alert and too alive to go into deep or moody contemplation.

By controlling their remarkable flare, choosing the right associates and trusting them, Gemini persons can aim for the finer things of life and gain them with the same ease that they capture the caprices of the moment.

VARIATIONS OF THE GEMINI SIGN

As Gemini folk have variable natures, so does their Twin Sign show marked extremes and sometimes fantastic differences among individuals with Birth Dates that may be very close together. However, the overall pattern always seems highly predominant.

Two Gemini people may have a hundred and one striking differences, variance of interests, etc., yet will be so similar fundamentally that they will strike exactly the same note, which may prove to be a chord of mutual mistrust.

For in their quick, Mercurian way, they use every possible device to eliminate rivalry and competition, usually by keeping ahead of the game.

THE EARLY PERIOD

Here, the Gemini person has all the advantage of the Taurus power. When quick schemes promise a fruition, the Gemini of this period can drive through and clinch them. These are the people who can really close a sale in forceful fashion.

They have a Venusian sympathy that aids the working of their clever Mercurian minds. They are smart at saying the right things at the right time. Here you will find persuasive natures packed with power.

Often, they become such sheer opportunists that people begin to doubt their promises. They are quick at thinking up excuses, then driving in for a new kill.

THE LATE PERIOD

Here, the quick, versatile nature of Gemini shows its greatest power of persuasion, particularly with those who are dealing with the opposite sex. Gemini persons of this period show all the changeability of the Moon and adopt the sensitive self-effacing manner associated with the Crab Sign.

They copy it because they are keen enough to note the success that the Crab brings. But let the Twins blow their bugle call to action and like Mercury, these people will take wing. Their Gemini traits then come completely to the fore.

Here again, results may vary as greatly as the Gemini traits. Once these people show themselves fickle, their past efforts may prove futile. On the contary, their way of winning sympathy enables them to start all over.

The Sign of
CANCER

CANCER: THE CRAB
(June 21–July 22)

			JUNE			
SUN	MON	TUE	WED	THU	FRI	SAT
	1	2	3	4	5	6
7	8	9	10	11	12	13
14	15	16	17	18	19	20
21	22	23	24	25	26	27
28	29	30				

			JULY			
SUN	MON	TUE	WED	THU	FRI	SAT
			1	2	3	4
5	6	7	8	9	10	11
12	13	14	15	16	17	18
19	20	21	22	23	24	25
26	27	28	29	30	31	

Birth Stone:	Ruby or Onyx
Birth Flower:	Water Lily or Larkspur
Harmonious Colors:	Green and Russet
Ruling Planet:	The Moon
Best Marriages:	Libra, Scorpio, Capricorn Pisces

This Sign of the Crab is appropriately as unnoticeable in the heavens as the creature it is supposed to represent. It is difficult to trace the outline of a crab from the faint stars which compose the constellation. This raises the assumption that it may have been so-named, because, like the crab, it has a retiring disposition that makes it very hard to find at night.

Indeed, the Constellation of Cancer might be said to be inconspicuous by its absence, so far as any outward brilliance is concerned. It would almost seem that the Ancients named the Sign, not from its appearance but from a study of the persons born beneath its rule.

For the Crab folk have a cautious, self-effacing way which often causes them to be greatly under-rated. They are shy because they are sensitive, but their attitude of self-withdrawal enables them to spend their time in deep contemplation that can bring fantastic results.

A sign of Success

The Crab Sign has its secret. In one word, it spells Success. If such persons can either curb their moody trends and harness their restless, changeable proclivities, they can rise to the highest notch in commerce and in terms of worldly achievement.

At the same time, many of this Sign are fervent in their urge for higher things, directing their contemplations toward philosophical or religious paths. In these, as well as in political or business matters, once they have formed what they regard as a solid or final opinion, they seldom if ever change it.

This is attributable to an ultra-conservatism found in persons born under this Sign. They want to be right before they go ahead; for that very reason, once they have instituted anything, they will meet all opposition.

When their sails are set, so are their minds, but only where the main course is concerned. On minor matters, they are changeable, their spirits ebbing and flowing like the tide.

They seek new scenes and are swayed by a desire for travel, but the best part of their going away is the coming home. For these folk are home lovers, homebodies and home makers. They are governed by emotions, which like the travel urge may grip them in an irresistable way.

Yet there seem to be underlying instincts beneath the influence of the Crab Sign, much as the crab itself seeks shelter, yet forays when occasion calls. These people are both acquisitive and tenacious, but those traits can be laid to an innate fear.

Conscious of their own sensitivity and shortcomings, watching fly-by-night methods forge ahead while they are starting a slow plod toward a distant goal, Crab folk have much to worry over and wonder about.

They accept the fable of the plodding tortoise that overtook the swift hare who slept by the roadside, but they are not confident it will work with them.

When swayed by visions of poverty, misery and neglect, they can become frantic and fritter away whatever possibilities they may possess. But that same fear prompts them to concentrate on plans that bring security.

Special Examples

Such simple beginnings can grow to tremendous proportions. One example was the vast success of John Wanamaker, who was born under this Sign, and the way he pyramided his idea of a department store into a great merchandising institution.

Another person born under this Sign was John D. Rockefeller, whose one great interest, oil, grew to the world's most gigantic industry.

Two Presidents of the United States were born under this Sign, more than 100 years apart. Yet both exhibited the same staid traits of patience and conservatism.

One was John Quincy Adams, the only man who followed his father's footsteps to the presidency and who remained a statesman until his death, at the ripe age of 81.

The other was Calvin Coolidge, who came up from a farm boy through the vice-presidency to attain the nation's highest office.

Adams was known as "Old Man Eloquence" while Coolidge was aptly nicknamed "Silent Cal," showing the wide range of the Crab Sign nature. But is also illustrates the singleness of purpose which is the feature of this Sign.

These persons set themselves a pattern, or like an architect, draw up a blueprint that can be followed through to its conclusion. Come rain or shine, hell or high-water, they will ride through it, when so equipped.

What to Avoid or Cultivate

But without such guidance, they are as changeable as the weather itself. Rain, cold, sunshine, even the dark of the moon, can produce a marked effect upon the moodier of Crab dispositions.

They must avoid jealousy, spite, mistrust and above all, fear of the future. If they feel the urge for a change of scene or occupation, they should curb it, at least until they have thought it over during another mood.

The more that these persons do for others, the more they will benefit themselves. That, strangely enough, is the crux of the Crab Sign.

VARIATIONS OF THE CANCER SIGN

The very changeability of the Crab Sign, which has its phases, like the Moon, produces a marked difference in the persons born beneath it.

With such persons, these differences are to be expected. Unless they flow with the tide and let their imaginative traits have proper leeway, they may restrict their natural ability.

Highly important is:

THE EARLY PERIOD

Here, the Sign of the Crab finds its greatest possibilities. Persons born in this period have changeable natures, but with a quick Mercurian touch, carried over from the sign of Gemini.

Swayed by the Moon, carried by its compelling power, the individual of this period may suddenly switch to the influence of Mercury, the mystery planet and capture its quick activation.

At this period we find people who are truly phenomenal. For years they may show their adaptability, their willingness to go along with the lunar changes. They may even be dependent, regarded as flighty.

Yet all the while, they have been nursing that Mercurian heritage that is truly theirs. When the time comes, they will assert it, because they never miss a trick. The contemplative, home-loving, accumulative nature of Cancer, given a proper dash of Gemini, is a mixture par excellence.

THE LATE PERIOD

Here, the conservative trend of the Crab nature is constantly being coaxed out into the open by the Sun-loving Sign of Leo. How well this works is a question. Just as the Moon reflects the Sun, so does the Crab Sign glow under such an urge.

But there must be time for meditation, a retirement into one's own shell. Otherwise persons born at this time will find themselves mentally and physically exhausted, unable to meet the demands that they try to fulfill.

♌

The Sign of
LEO

LEO: THE LION
(July 22–August 22)

JULY						
SUN	MON	TUE	WED	THU	FRI	SAT
			1	2	3	4
5	6	7	8	9	10	11
12	13	14	15	16	17	18
19	20	21	22	23	24	25
26	27	28	29	30	31	

AUGUST						
SUN	MON	TUE	WED	THU	FRI	SAT
						1
2	3	4	5	6	7	8
9	10	11	12	13	14	15
16	17	18	19	20	21	22
23	24	25	26	27	28	29

Birth Stone:	Sardonyx or Peridot
Birth Flower:	Gladiolus or Poppy
Harmonious Colors:	Red and Orange
Ruling Planet:	The Sun
Best Marriages:	Aries, Libra, Sagittarius, Aquarius

The Sign of the Lion denotes an impulsive, exuberant nature, filled with courage, spirit and determination. No Sign of the Zodiac offers greater opportunity than Leo, with its mighty, forceful willpower often to the fore.

The question is: Can the Leo individual come up to all that his Birth Sign promises? Often, he can, but only by controlling his own overpowering impulses.

Even then, the Leo nature usually rises to an imperious magnitude. Witness the fact that Napoleon was born under this sign and did not stop until his imperial ambitions were attained.

Remember, too, that Napoleon met his Waterloo. The saying that "Pride goeth before a fall" applies indeed to persons with Leonine proclivities. For theirs is the proudest Sign of the Zodiac, conspicuous because of Regulus, the Kingly Star.

Yet singularly, at one period of the year, showers of meteors issue from the direction of the constellation Leo. These falling stars, called Leonids, could very well represent the ambitious persons of this Sign who failed to reach the high status of mighty Regulus.

Attainment of Ambition

Fortunately, all Leo folk are not victims of their own ambitions. If they use their persuasive powers in a pleasant way, they will find them a potent force indeed. Leo people can create confidence by their very manner and if they back it with the action that they promise, they will ride high, wide and handsome.

Never, however, should they exhibit too much enthusiasm. It is apt to be mistaken for egotism. The Leo individual, when sure that he can accomplish anything, has a way of saying so. Listeners who lack the Leo vigor may doubt these claims and refuse to go along.

Thus Leo claims may be classed as empty boasts, with the public ready to adopt an attitude of "I told you so," every time the Leo person fails to come through.

Leo folk should remember the proverb that "Rome was not built in a day." Along with their impetuous desire to accomplish things, they magnify their own ability, setting themselves impossible tasks, another step toward disaster.

Being natural leaders, they should seek opportunities to display that ability, particularly as they resent taking commands from others. But Leo folk should not let an urge for independence carry them on odd trails where they will uselessly waste their vigor.

Development of the Leo Nature

The higher their authority or position, the more they can display the Leonine dignity that so impresses all who meet them. The Leo person who curbs his impulse until the time to act has arrived, will virtually have victory in his grasp.

From this it would seem that the lion-hearted person born beneath this Sign would have everything to gain by sitting back and waiting to display his strength. But no lion ever won a battle by issuing hollow roars from within a lair.

Unless the Leo type can show that impulse, flash that power and impress people with his pride, he may become lazy, conceited and even resort to the boasts that he should so carefully avoid.

Well-developed, the Leo nature is one of love and loyalty, gaining reciprocation and appreciation from others. They can sway public sympathy and are masters at winning friends and influencing people.

But this requires a radiant manner, a warmth of fine feeling, a true generosity toward one and all. Otherwise, Leonine attempts at leadership will be classed as arrogance. In turn, the Leo nature may become sullen and revengeful.

Actually, the Leo nature craves luxury and refinement, the proper accompaniments of a kingly poise. Those can not be gained by impulsive action or forceful demand. Here, the Leo influence and persuasion must be exerted to the full.

What to Avoid or Cultivate

Leo people help themselves by helping others. They should remember the fable of the Lion and the Mouse. In that story, the lion was kindly to a tiny mouse, who later reciprocated by gnawing the strands of a net in which the mighty jungle king was snared.

Often, a person of the impetuous, imperious Leo type is too prone to disregard retiring, mousey individuals, who some time might prove themselves friends indeed.

For retreat is foreign to the Leo nature. If their impetuosity carries them too far, they must make the best of it. That is when they need help. Unless they gain followers, they can not show the leadership which is their forte.

Incentive is helpful to the Leo impulse. Along with the recognition that they must venture in order to gain, these people should strive to be good losers in order to be recognized as worthy winners.

Along with controlling their own ego, they must not only avoid anger; they must remain immune to flattery. Such points observed, they should gain more than their share of the world, if they restrain themselves from wanting all of it.

VARIATIONS OF THE LEO SIGN

That lion-hearted exuberance which characterizes Leo is found in nearly every Birth Date of the Sign. Indeed, of all the Signs of the Zodiac, this is the most consistent. You know a Leo the moment you encounter one, though it must be said that the domineering quality may be the one that most forcibly expresses itself.

Peculiar qualities are observable in Leo, none the less. That is specially noticeable in:

THE EARLY PERIOD

Persons born in the first few days, or even the first week of the Leo period have all the brilliance that is connected with the Lion Sign. The big point is: How will they display it?

Leo is usually untrammeled, free, influential. On that account they show a natural intuition and are masters of any situation. In the broad light of open day, they assert themselves in a truly sunny style.

But the early category shows a proclivity for combining intuition with imagination. These persons feel that it is their duty to bring things from the dark of the moon and display them in open sunlight.

This can raise them to great heights, if they are lucky enough to be championing a right cause. But is can drop them to depths of despondency if they waste their Leo exuberance in unworthy effort.

THE LATE PERIOD

In the last few days of this Sign, Leo can show other problems, too. Though such persons are kindly of manner, friendly of disposition, their impulsive nature may take on an analytical trend. They are apt to become picayune, too demanding in a small way.

Always, it behooves the Leo nature to be itself, strong, stout-hearted and above whatever may reduce the natural grandeur of this Sign to petty policies.

♍

The Sign of
VIRGO

VIRGO: THE VIRGIN
(August 22–September 23)

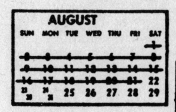

Birth Stone:	Sapphire, Chrysolite or Pink Jasper
Birth Flower:	Aster, Morning Glory or Cornflower
Harmonious Colors:	Black, Gold and Brown
Ruling Planet:	Mercury
Best Marriages:	Aries, Taurus, Capricorn, Pisces

This is the Sign of the analytical mind, quick to note facts, capable of retaining them and prone to lose itself in a maze of detail.

By nature, the Virgo temperament is very orderly, wanting everything in its proper place, and demanding spick-and-span surroundings to a point where it becomes an obsession.

Others, unable to organize or simplify their affairs due to pressure of work and business demands, develop a system of mental pigeon-holes which can prove fantastic.

In either case, they may worry themselves with fine points or become so bogged down with detail that they find themselves forced to efforts far beyond the reward that they receive in return.

This is because the quick-minded Virgo person frequently takes the hard way as the easy way. They have inquiring minds, are avid readers and frequently possess a photographic memory to an uncanny degree. Mental tasks which many other people regard as formidable, may prove commonplace to the Virgo person.

An Adaptive Mentality

Often, however, they take credit for originating ideas that they have simply adapted from things that they have seen or heard about. Often, this is an unconscious action on their part, their minds automatically sorting and linking ideas with great rapidity. But they are generally able to point out sources from which other persons picked up presumably new ideas or notions.

Their urge for analysis and detail causes Virgo persons to appreciate many clever touches or trivial points that other people would pass by entirely. On the contrary, such trifles may bother them badly.

Often neat as well as orderly, Virgo persons make good impressions and, in their turn, are often impressed by important personages. They will go out of their way to curry favors with bigwigs, but here again the action may be of an unconscious sort. The Virgo mind recognizes automatically that it will find more to analyze through such associations and is grateful for the opportunity.

Seldom, however, do Virgo folk indulge in flattery; their minds are too exacting for that. But they are clever as well as critical and use tact when occasion demands. They like to dig up odd facts and pass them along to interested parties.

Vagaries of Virgo

As a result, the Virgo person may be too talkative for his own good. They may bore people with too much detail and reveal too much about themselves in the bargain. Having quick minds, they are often fast talkers, priding themselves on their ability as extemporaneous speakers.

But if they listen to tape recordings of their own voice, their critical natures would, enable them to recognize and correct some of their own flaws. They would agree that they should think over what they intend to say before they proceed to say it.

For Virgo people are their own taskmasters. They see through sham because they are perfectionists. They take criticism as readily as they give it, but are quick to excuse their own shortcomings.

That is because they analyze themselves as well as others. In their self-analysis, they take the view that they are doing things the right way, because they would not be satisfied with any other way; but with this proviso:

They allow for personal problems, lack of time, money or appreciation—anything that adds up to their own advantage and marks them as big time. Often, this makes them the target of ridicule, even among their friends.

Yet this, too, is explainable by Virgo standards. They force themselves to be optimists, to believe in themselves, rather than knock themselves down through their own analysis. They become self-centered as a form of self-sacrifice.

What to Avoid or Cultivate

But don't be sorry for the Virgo crew. That's their way of getting fun out of life. If they didn't plague themselves with a deluge of detail, they would be victims of imaginary ills and problems.

Meanwhile, they can worry other people to the limit, without realizing it. When they begin to criticize their friends and moan over their own problems, they make themselves unpopular. Virgo people want their way and, if they don't get it, they wll lie right down and quit.

But first, they will try to make themselves

indispensable, even if they work themselves to a frazzle doing it. They can't be wrong without being right. This makes them very difficult indeed. They even find it difficult to take advice, because their specialty is giving it.

Virgo people are modest, but often to a fault. If they showed self-importance, they would be unable to claim that they were not appreciated.

VARIATIONS OF THE VIRGO SIGN

Though Virgo persons may vary vastly in likes and dislikes, running the gamut from the most energetic to the most conservative of natures, those analytical minds of theirs have figured what they want in terms of what they can get and that attainment is their real aim.

The quick way in which two Virgo individuals can recognize each other's problems and either offer suggestions or let them go their way, is proof of this. Those Mercurian minds are alert to all phases and seldom miss a trick.

Perhaps the greatest variance is found in:

THE EARLY PERIOD

Here, the Virgo nature, which gathers in so

much, is able to absorb much of the brilliance and fiery spirit of Leo, often utilizing it to fine purpose.

Such Virgo folk are much like plants or trees so situated that they can catch the full sunlight in the afternoon, flourishing accordingly. But as we move into the first week of the Sign, the amount dwindles proportionately.

Then we find persons whose quick minds are fretful, due to frustrated thoughts of fame which they did not gain, yet which they feel should be theirs. Their Mercurian minds are right on that point, which makes it all the worse.

Outdoor life, plenty of sunlight, sports like fishing and boating, anything that tunes them to Nature will supply through physical ways the yearnings which they mentally crave.

THE LATE PERIOD

In total contrast to the Early Period, the departing days of Virgo produce a personality that balances the factors that it analyzes. The Mercurian quickness, softened by Venusian love of harmony and beauty, guides these individuals into paths of kindness and beauty.

What they acquire through Virgo quickness, they put on the scales of Libra to value it fairly instead of trusting to their own judgment which is often too rapid to be right.

With mental weighed against physical, logic balanced with sincerity, Virgo persons closest to the Libra line have huge opportunities indeed, but only if they give the finer phases of their nature full reign.

The Sign of
LIBRA

LIBRA: THE SCALES
(September 23–October 23)

Birth Stone:	Opal or Tourmaline
Birth Flower:	Marigold (Calendula) or Dahlia
Harmonious Colors:	Blue and Yellow Also: Black and White
Ruling Planet:	Venus
Best Marriages:	Aries, Leo, Sagittarius Frequently with: Gemini, Aquarius Conflicting Signs: Virgo, Pisces

This Sign, which represents the Scales, is a symbol of balance, which represents a constant attempt to equalize the situations of life.

This does not mean that persons born under this Sign are qualified to sit in judgment of themselves as well as others. On the contrary, Libra folk may be the most mixed up of all.

The figure of Justice holds the scales, endeavoring to balance them. But Justice herself is blindfolded. That is often true of those born under Libra. If they could trust their own judgment, they wouldn't need the scales.

As a result, they are very sympathetic and understanding, anxious to learn the views of others. But they assume that these are given with the same sincerity in which they are accepted. This means that Libra persons, like the scales themselves, are very easily swayed.

The problem comes in balancing up. The old saying, "Everyone knows that 2 and 2 make 4," has been amended by the modern quip, "Yes, but sometimes they make 22."

That is what can happen with the Libra sense of judgment, when all their sympathy, generosity, charity and self-sacrifice are tossed on one side of the scales.

The Sign of Intuition

Their intuition is phenomenal. They can recognize things instinctively, telling true from false, good from bad. The saying, "First thoughts are best," is one that they are constantly proving and those are the impressions that they automatically balance. But when they begin to add other facts or amend their opinions, they lose that delicacy of touch.

The advice of friends, their own worry over problems, a craving for excitement that seems innate, are factors that can disturb their balanced natures, often causing them to go in opposition to their own interests and lose the advantage of their intuitive power.

Similarly, they can magnify trifles, adding 2 and 2 to 22, instead of only 4. Some instinctive aversion, some slighting remark or unkind thing coming from another person, may trouble the Libra nature to no end. Such things lead to rifts.

For the Libra individual is so sincere, so soulful, so self-sacrificing, so completely wrapped in the lives of others, that they expect others to be the same. Ambition, business, all the practical side of life can go out the window, when the affairs of family, friends or humanity are at stake.

Well-Weighed Factors

Given a choice betwen two factors, Libra will always gravitate to the human rather than the practical. They are ruled by instinct more than reason. Often they lavish affection upon those who do not deserve it and they are frequently blinded by their own sympathy.

You will hear Libra folk paint wonderful pictures of members of their family or friends; upon meeting the persons in question, you will find that they fall far short of such specifications. All those wonderful virtues were simply built up in the Libra mind.

This goes with the Libra trait of always siding with the underdog. Libra folk are so afraid that justice will miscarry, that they will join a wrong cause simply to make sure it gets a hearing. Then, all the argument in the world will simply make them all the more stubborn.

They take up new ideas in the same way, often showing trust in strangers who proceed to sell them short. When criticized or even questioned on this score, Libra persons become bitter and angry. This confounds the critic, who can not understand why Libra rebels at logic.

The reason, of course, is the depth of Libra's own nature. They never want to be reminded when their intuition fails. That is one of their touchiest traits; but there is another that is also difficult to detect.

That is the Libra pride of possession. Libra folk are self-sacrificing and sentimental toward others to such a great extent that gradually they gain an ingrown sense of domination. They express confidence in others, hopeful that those people will go along with Libra when the time arrives. The more subordinate they appear to be, the more independent they become.

This leads to breaks in business, romance and even family affairs. Anything may cause this, a recurrent argument, constant shift of plans, even careless actions that may disturb the exacting Libra nature.

What to Avoid or Cultivate

Quite paradoxically, harmonious, home-loving Libra persons may become horribly unhappy in the very setting that they did so much to create. They hate to see others simply take all that for granted.

That is, if Libra folk can actually "hate" anything. Even after an outright break, they still feel sorry for the other fellow. You can always appeal to the Libra personality by honestly adapting yourself to their sympathetic moods.

Neglected, Libra persons become morose and dissatisfied, so it is good policy not to neglect them. Find and share their common interests, music, art, sports, even mere conviviality and harmony will reign supreme.

VARIATIONS OF THE LIBRA SIGN

Life, to Libra, is so much a matter of balancing up, that the differences in persons of this Sign can become striking indeed. Yet, always they seek balance, one way or another.

The sympathy inspired by Venus causes the full-strained Libra type to apply this to all human affairs, so you find them always making allowances, whether logical or not.

Thus Libra persons will generally sympathize

with one another, no matter how wide apart their interests. Sharper lines of demarcation are found in the fringes of this Sign, as witness:

THE EARLY PERIOD

Picking up facts as well as fancies with speed and precision, the Libra person of this early period analyzes them in Virgo fashion and tosses them into the balance.

In this way, they come to swifter and more logical decisions than in any other portion of the period. Other members of the Libra tribe may accept first sentiments intuitively, or hedge for the same reason.

But these first-weekers can often justify their attitude to the finest point. As a result, they may display a fascinating charm; quick, ready minds; with an amazing aptitude at solving the problems of others.

But if they can't balance their own affairs, they may resort to wild hunches or shady Mercurian tactics. Persons of this period should seek balance first; analysis afterward.

THE LATE PERIOD

Here we find Libra persons who justify things in their own mind; then put them into action regardless. They have the Martian flare found in the upcoming Scorpio Sign, with a definite determination.

They become secretly possessive of whatever they once owned, feeling that it still is theirs. Anything they add to the balance, they want to keep. They figure that whatever is right is worth fighting for and they may even provoke a battle simply to justify a claim.

Spite and jealousy may be exhibited by such people, if they feel that a worthy goal is an end that can be justified by such means.

♏

The Sign of
SCORPIO

SCORPIO: THE SCORPION
(October 23–November 21)

Birth Stone:	Topaz or Malachite
Birth Flower:	Chrysanthemum or Red Carnation
Harmonious Colors:	Crimson and Ultramarine (Deep Blue)
Ruling Planet:	Mars
Best Marriages:	Taurus, Cancer, Pisces Sometimes with: Leo, Virgo

This is the Sign of the great outdoors, the symbol of the true nature lover. Here we find rugged individualists, who will not be stopped once they feel that they have embarked upon a rightful enterprise.

The term "scorpion" is appropriate for this Sign, when taken in a broad, individualistic sense. As living creatures, scorpions adapt themselves to many conditions and they are quick and sharp in attack.

From the scorpion's viewpoint, all this is natural and justifiable, even to the poison sting which some deliver to their enemies and prey.

This applies to the Scorpio individual as well. Among persons born under this, we find ardent crusaders, bold adventurers, fearless fighters. They are willing to take risks which would appall many other people.

Often, those risks are calculated, which accounts for Scorpio's success. But here we strike the crux of the Scorpio nature. The higher the Scorpio intellectuality, the more worthy its purposes and the better and more effective its plans.

Scorpio attacks shrewdly, not blindly. These persons watch for opportune moments to deliver their drive, seldom switching from one tack to another. In accord with that policy, they keep their ideas to themselves, using the element of surprise as a factor in their favor.

A Sign of Self-Control

Along with this, they have self-control, a progressive nature, and a practical intuition. Scorpio persons can size a situation as no one else can, particularly when action is required. They seem to know instinctively what other people will do and they make allowance for it.

Their self-control keeps them from being impulsive. Contrarily, their urge for action does not allow them to become long-range planners. They meet issues as they find them, confident that one success will lead to another.

From this it would seem that Scorpio people have an edge on the remainder of the Zodiac, but say not so. They can be their own worst enemies, without even beginning to realize it. Tact is not in their department. They bait people who oppose them.

This works well when they are confronted by stupid people, or those who have real reason to fear the Scorpio wrath. But Scorpio's secretive manner is a give-away to keener minds, who often find ways to counteract a Scorpio campaign.

The more limited the Scorpio viewpoint, education or experience, the more such a person must curtail his field of activity. This is not true of other Signs, where unusual quickness, talents and abiding qualities are found.

A Secretive Nature

The Scorpio nature involves concentration, a strictly selfish outlook that must be expanded to gain success. Secrecy is naturally accompanied by suspicion; here, again, a broad outlook and wide experience are elements needed toward development of the higher Scorpio nature.

Scorpio folk are a law unto themselves. They can take hardship, go through any ordeal. They expect reward for effort, in the form of the things, they like and want. If they should cultivate a taste for better things, they will accordingly further their self-development in order to get them.

Otherwise, the Scorpio personality remains limited indeed. It is a temperament suited to a prospector, a small rancher, miner, or skipper of a fishing boat, who can set the pace for a compact crew of subordinates along a definitely established line.

Similarly, women of this Sign are shrewd buyers rather than good sellers. They can handle small enterprises or specialized departments. Along with Scorpio's practical intuition, there is the quality of practical sympathy. Scorpio people, above those of all other Signs, can keep a secret. That adds to the confidence they create.

What to Avoid or Cultivate

But the limited Scorpio nature is satisfied with food, drink and other mundane pleasures. A Scorpio person can become quarrelsome in private life, trying to rule family and friends. Scorpio needs more outlets, bigger responsibilities, along with self-expansion.

A shining example of the Scorpio type was the famous Will Rogers, who started in vaudeville with a rope-twirling act, added a few homespun comments as a fill-in and eventually became the leading humorist and most popular personality of his time.

Will Rogers sounded the keynote of his success in the statement, "I never met a man I didn't like." That is a good phrase for Scorpio folk to adopt as their motto. They can rise to great heights artistically, commercially, financially and politically, provided they prove themselves worthy of the honors that they gain.

They will do this through exercising self-restraint along with their virile natures and directing their deep-set minds toward the progress that they preach. Above all, they will do it by making friends, not enemies.

VARIATIONS OF THE SCORPIO SIGN

The lusty, loyal, lively Scorpio nature is as subject to as many individual types as is Nature itself. Some may be stormy, others calm and serene, or they may even switch from one tempo to the other.

But in purpose, stick-to-it tactics and the willingness to meet steel with steel, the Scorpio nature is consistent, whether or not it fights for good or bad. Often, the Scorpio individual can prove cunning, selfish and unscrupulous, with the Martian nature taking full control.

This is strongly tempered in:

THE EARLY PERIOD

Here, with Libra as a backlog, the Scorpio temperament is definitely geared to justice. Powerful crusaders and reformers come from this period, which is strongly humanitarian due to the Libra sentiment.

The policy advocated by Teddy Roosevelt: "Speak softly, tread gently, but carry a big stick!" is highly descriptive of this period. Early Scorpio persons have a way of rising above criticism and standing ready to back their convictions.

But the Scorpio nature usually stands predominant, not only in this Early Period but in:

THE LATE PERIOD

Combining the Scorpio nature with the straight aim of Sagittarius, a person born at this time can rise to any attainment. Such persons have force, strength and determination, so all they need is a goal.

That, plus the fact that a curbing of their Martian spirit will help them sway the public with their Jupiterian influence and appeal. Remember: This period is still basically Scorpio; therefore it may prove too challenging for its own good.

Rather than trying to knock down all the opposition in sight, these persons should stress the fullness of their nature, developing themselves along humanitarian lines, always with a high objective.

The Sign of
SAGITTARIUS

SAGITTARIUS: THE BOWMAN
(November 22–December 21)

Birth Stone:	Turquoise or Zircon Also: Lapis Lazuli
Birth Flower:	Poinsettia or Holly Also: Narcissus
Harmonious Colors:	Mauve, Indigo and Green
Ruling Planet:	Jupiter
Best Marriages:	Aries Gemini, Leo, Libra Sometimes Own Sign: Sagittarius

This is the Sign of the Bowman, the straight shooter who never misses the mark. Here are people who are direct, purposeful and filled with vision. They have a happy nature because they are independent and thereby disinclined to worry and fritter over many things that would cause trouble and create problems in the lives of other persons.

Sagittarius persons are adherents of the rule, "Honesty is the best Policy" and usually follow it to the letter. They have no reason to brag about this, as it is largely an underlying trait, an out-crop of their "straight shooting" nature.

Being independent, those of the Sagittarius Sign are also carefree. They advise others to be the same way and are therefore a great help— sometimes.

Their jolt comes when they find themselves misunderstood, accused of running other people's affairs—which they certainly do not!— or marked as reformers out to change the world.

It is simply that the Sagittarius person must think straight to shoot straight. They become a source of annoyance and despair to friends who want to weigh matters, compromise, judge by appearances, etc.; all things which are abhorrent to the Bowman's nature.

Setting a Standard

An individual of the Sagittarius type may set himself up as a standard quite unconsciously. He never realizes that he is aiming for marks that others can not hope to hit. They can't even pull the bowstring, let alone loose the arrow.

By virtue of his very independence, the Bowman lets himself in for criticism and even ridicule. He may buy the finest gems or art treasures, or show fine taste in minor things; yet all the while be careless of his appearance, wearing shabby clothes with pockets lined in cash.

Yet, in utter contradiction, such persons may decide to "put on the dog" and make a great show, never realizing that they may be out of character from one day to the next.

How can that be explained in such straightforward natures?

Simply because Sagittarius boils down to one word: Purpose. They truly believe that "What's worth doing at all, is worth doing well."

Dress, appearance, sociability, may be necessary to some Bowman's aim, yet at the same time only incidental. That is when Bowman—or his feminine counterpart—will blossom out in full glory.

Don't get the wrong notion that Sagittarius persons have strictly one-track minds. Far from it! Often, they can do anything to which they may put those minds of theirs. But it is not in their nature to switch, especially when they are aiming for a given target.

But give your Sagittarius person a hobby with time to devote to it; show him a task which he will regard as essential to his major aim. You will see him score a bull's-eye on that target with his usual marksman's facility.

Honesty and Confidence

Being honest, persons born under this Sign are also truthful—perhaps too truthful. They speak frankly, even bluntly, but their words may carry a sharp barb. They dislike deception on the part of others and often make them the targets of their wrath.

The vision found in persons of the Sagittarius type is notable for its foresight, but usually fails to take in the vast surrounding panorama. Confident of their aim, they positively predict how a certain thing will come out, if it is simple enough to appraise.

But complex conditions are beyond them. When they leave something for some one else to do, or rely entirely on that person's judgment, it is apt to go awry—unless the other person was also born under Sagittarius or some harmonious Sign.

Concentration is the keynote of Sagittarius, but in a practical way. These people become actors, financiers and statesmen. They gain public esteem through their integrity and their careers consist of hitting one bull's-eye after another. But they set their sights on new targets as well.

What to Avoid or Cultivate

They know how to make money but will skimp if they feel it necessary. Thus with all their wealth, some rich persons of this Sign are painfully penurious. Extravagance is almost absent in this Sign, though such people may spend fortunes on worth-while things.

This is because they have a strong sense of values, which they apply to people as well as things, making enemies as well as friends. Those born under Sagittarius should curb their wit and general expressions of opinion, rather than hurt others with sharp prods, even though the barbs may be deserved.

Otherwise, the Sagittarius individual will become a critical, short-tempered, even slothful person, hiding whatever talent he may possess.

VARIATIONS OF THE SAGITTARIUS SIGN

There is one saying that all of the Bowman Sign can well remember: "Not failure, but low aim, is a fault."

In the starry heavens, the fanciful figure of the Bowman, Sagittarius, is aiming his shaft at the Eagle, otherwise Aquila. This symbolizes the Bowman seeking to hit the highest mark attainable.

Study those born under Sagittarius and you will note how their happiness hinges on their aim. Also, you will find many who have let mere flights of fancy draw them from a true target.

When aimless, the Bowman is helpless. That plight seldom occurs to those born in:

THE EARLY PERIOD

With Sagittarius and its active, jovial mentality grasping the physical urge of Scorpio, you find a vivacity that can not be matched by any other Sign or combination.

These people gather knowledge, then use it to a purpose. Gifted with insight, often robust or unrestrained in nature, they add the Martian drive to their other assets, often with great results.

They can take on huge burdens and still win out, but show restraint, keeping their drive subservient to their fundamental trait of coolness and aim. Otherwise, they may overshoot the mark.

THE LATE PERIOD

Here, the Bowman's nature tends toward the intellectual. The closer the Sagittarius type comes to the verge of Capricorn, the more he will appreciate culture and philosophy.

Such persons will not be satisfied with mere

physical or commercial accomplishments. They should set their aim early for high marks in scholarly and educational lines. Truly, they can aim for the stars.

The Sign of
CAPRICORN

CAPRICORN: THE GOAT
(December 21–January 20)

DECEMBER

SUN	MON	TUE	WED	THU	FRI	SAT
		1	2	3	4	5
6	7	8	9	10	11	12
13	14	15	16	17	18	19
20	21	22	23	24	25	26
27	28	29	30	31		

JANUARY

SUN	MON	TUE	WED	THU	FRI	SAT
					1	2
3	4	5	6	7	8	9
10	11	12	13	14	15	16
17	18	19	20	21	22	23
24	25	26	27	28	29	30

Birth Stone:	Garnet or Onyx
Birth Flower:	Snowdrop or White Carnation
Harmonious Colors:	Violet, Purple, Black and Silver Gray
Ruling Planet:	Saturn
Best Marriages:	Aries, Taurus, Cancer, Virgo

This is the Sign of the Goat, the most conservative in the Zodiac and unquestionably one of the finest. Here we find persons who are patient, plodding, yet at the same time solid and substantial.

The Goat folk encounter many ups and downs, if only because they are so conscientious and sincere. They can become determined to the point where they are stubborn, but not through animosity.

They simply can't abide being the "goat" over a long period and in true goat fashion, they will try to butt their way out of an unhappy situation. Often, they are successful in this, for a very simple reason; namely:

Many of their problems are of their own making. If they avoided such problems, or rebelled against them sooner, they would get the same results. But the Capricorn clan goes right on taking it, giving their friends and associates the false notion that they are satisfied with things as they are.

Then, bam!, comes an outburst so sudden and effective in its drive, that it becomes the Capricorn pattern. This varies, of course, with individuals. Some persons of this type develop a challenging attitude and literally butt into situations, or show such a tendency. But the majority shows more restraint, going into action only after due provocation.

The Need for Confidence

With restraint, perseverance is another Capricorn attribute. Like the goat, a person of this Sign will clamber up steep paths to reach new pinnacles, often taking the hardest and steepest way.

Though anxious to manage their own affairs, Goat folk frequently are lacking in self-confidence, particularly after they have experienced dire results or have been subjected to undeserved periods of poverty.

When they become too self-conscious, they are inclined to turn moody and go into glum reflections on the past. Oddly, they find solitude a good way of pulling out of such unhappy states.

This may hinge on the fact that Capricorn persons are introspective in a practical way, because they are largely aware of their shortcomings and are prepared to do something about them. Thinking things over helps to rally the Capricorn nature.

Again, the true Capricorn person is very quick to spot flattery or false praise and discount them. So those born under this Sign take their own opinions rather than free advice of so-called friends.

An Abiding Nature

Being truly kindly and self-sacrificing, Capricorn persons can become morose over the loss of loved ones. It is hard for them to dispel clouds of gloom or thoughts of death. Often, they find solace in art, music, or other finer things in which they are frequently talented.

Too, their ability to go on, plus their unwillingness to accept defeat, enable them to renew their energy and rise to still greater heights. They thrive on responsibility and, given the proper chance, Capricorn folk have become some of the most successful of all persons.

Their abiding natures, great understanding and keen sense of obligation have raised them to high levels in professions and in commerce. Study the career of Benjamin Franklin, with his rules for self-help, his persistence, patience and long-range philosophy; there you will find a fine example of Capricorn.

These persons are economical, sound in judgment and excellent organizers, which makes business their forte. Their ups usually carry them higher than their downs, thus their progress is continued over the years.

Long-range planning is to their order, often bringing them success in later life. What is more, they are apt to live long enough to enjoy it. Usually, these Goat folk continue to be active up to an advanced age.

What to Avoid or Cultivate

But their methodical ways and their reflective life make them very sensitive to criticism. Once someone has taken advantage of them, they are often too hurt to fight back. Too often, they let others take credit for things that they should rightfully claim.

These factors do much to drag down the Capricorn nature. Goat folk should not only trust themselves more, but should assert themselves. Being meditative, they do well to think out plans for things to come.

In brief, they should push themselves as they push others. Your true Capricorn always returns a favor. Therefore they should expect and get more for themselves. They can rise to great heights socially, politically and commercially, when they do.

But they must curb their own vanity. Each new pinnacle gives them a desire to exult. The higher the height, the more faithfully they should adhere to the rules that helped them gain that summit.

VARIATIONS IN THE CAPRICORN SIGN

There is so much of the mental in the Capricorn makeup that it might well be termed the Sign of Moods. That is why many people find the Capricorn nature difficult to understand.

Since their own moods worry them, they feel that those of the Goat folk should do the same. But, not so! The Capricorn clan feel sorry for themselves only as a means toward inspiration, strange as that may seem.

Out of solitude, they rise to success. From

melancholy, they attain mastery. This strain runs throughout the Sign but is modified in:

THE EARLY PERIOD

Coupled with the love for solemn, soulful things, the early Capricorn here is spurred by purpose. Meditation and music are kindred in the Capricorn nature. From them, they aspire to great heights, to which they can aim with the precision of Sagittarius.

Most people dread the influence of Saturn, consider it a baleful power. Not so the person born under Capricorn. Solitude and study are to them synonymous. Given the jovial, aspiring optimism of the Bowman, the Goat nature knows no bounds.

Many professional men benefit from this combination.

Lawyers, physicians, scientists acquire knowledge under the deep, meditative Sign of Capricorn; then, instead of bounding off to green pastures, they aim for bigger, better projects and score the Bowman's bull's-eye.

THE LATE PERIOD

Here, the contemplative nature of the Goat Sign is directed more toward social and humane affairs than to strictly individual achievement, though their artistry and commercial ability may be great indeed.

It is through the adaptability of their talents that they gain prestige, rather than by concentrating on a single target. These persons are fortunate in having many outlets and should try to develop them as a means of rising above disappointments or despondency.

The Sign of
AQUARIUS

AQUARIUS: THE WATER CARRIER
(January 20–February 19)

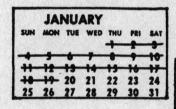

			JANUARY			
SUN	MON	TUE	WED	THU	FRI	SAT
				1	2	3
4	5	6	7	8	9	10
11	12	13	14	15	16	17
18	19	20	21	22	23	24
25	26	27	28	29	30	31

			FEBRUARY			
SUN	MON	TUE	WED	THU	FRI	SAT
1	2	3	4	5	6	7
8	9	10	11	12	13	14
15	16	17	18	19	20	21
22	23	24	25	26	27	28

Birth Stone:	Amethyst
Birth Flower:	Primrose or Violet
Harmonious Colors:	Light Blue, Nile Green, Yellow
Ruling Planet:	Saturn
Best Marriages:	Aries, Leo, Sagittarius Occasionally with: Gemini, Libra Doubtful With Own Sign: Aquarius

This is the Sign of the Water Carrier, the great humanitarian symbol of the Zodiac. Rudyard Kipling put its philosophy across in a truly grand way with his poem of Gunga Din, who was cursed and reviled, only to be recognized as a "better man" by the very one who had belted and flayed him.

How true that is of the Aquarian nature!

Four Presidents of the United States, William H. Harrison, Abraham Lincoln, William McKinley and Franklin D. Roosevelt were born under the Sign of Aquarius. Every one of them died in office, fitting testimony to the arduous way in which they met their tasks.

The Aquarian nature becomes fearless when an individual of this Sign is sure that he is right or has a fixed duty to perform. That was the philosophy of Gunga Din, who ran the gauntlet of the enemy's fire, carrying water to those who needed it.

An Aptitude for Achievement

Some of the greatest and most beloved persons in history have been born under Aquarius, because the world at large has not only recognized but sensed the humanitarian nature that these personages displayed.

But it is not all quite that simple.

Along with such commanding natures, Aquarius folk have the power of persuasion by means of direct, simple speech. They also display a personal magnetism that sways many whom they meet. Yet with it all, they are impersonal enough to switch from one individual to another, letting each feel the warmth of their friendship, or whatever they can give.

This is true of the lowliest Aquarian to the highest; from the mere Water Carrier who so appropriately signifies this Sign, up to the highest brackets. They are agreeable, yet reliable; active, yet calm; progressive, yet benevolent.

Much more could be said regarding the fulness of the Aquarius nature, but there are other phases to be considered. One important note is this:

Though the highly developed person of this Sign can rise to great fame despite seemingly insurmountable obstacles, the undeveloped Aquarius nature may never get off the ground.

The term "undeveloped" does not mean some one lacking in the Aquarian virtues. On the contrary you may meet such persons who are courteous, well-spoken, scholarly and even hypnotic in manner. Yet they may prove to be total losses in whatever work they have undertaken.

Acceptance of Advice

These people must learn to take criticism with acclaim. They can not afford to let their human sympathy deteriorate into mere maudlin sentiment. They should not injure their natural dignity by turning it into a display of self-importance.

Yet Aquarius folk do all such things. They love to talk about themselves, thinking it will impress people, which it does—the wrong way. They put their own affairs first, letting others wait instead of keeping appointments on time.

They ask advice and then proceed to disregard it. They show interest in people and promptly proceed to forget them. They talk about great opportunities, but do nothing to develop them. When they fail, they often blame other people.

Now the strange thing about the Aquarius type is that many of these traits are reasonably justified, at least in specific cases. A person may have things that he can say about himself. He may have lost out because some one imposed upon him.

But those aren't the things that people want to hear about. They are attracted by the Water Carrier because they think that he can do good for them. He must come up to their expectations in order to maintain their esteem.

What to Avoid or Cultivate

Those born under Aquarius must rise above their own personal interests and really give of themselves to others. Yet they must not trust the natures of those others as much as they do their own. A fine sense of discrimination is necessary to the Aquarius make-up.

Critics may call it hypocrisy, but they are wrong. Aquarius persons must allow for the doubtings of others in order to accomplish big things. Many of them find their life work in specialized lines, like invention, for they have inquiring minds. But there, too, they must recognize that they were meant for big things.

Minds are keen under this Sign. They can work from small things up to great. They know human nature, even if they sometimes trust it too far. They are good buyers, good sellers, with a rare wit and ready manner that goes far to further their ends while increasing their popularity.

But they can break themselves as well as make themselves. They have big ideas, but need the power to swing them. Such power is gained through action; not mere talk.

Step by step, the true Aquarian should develop his warmth of manner, show people that he can remember them as well as greet them and literally create the idea that he is bigger than he is, but not by merely saying so.

By counting, studying and activating all his assets, the Aquarius person can personally supply the difference between his own success or failure.

VARIATIONS OF THE AQUARIUS SIGN

The Aquarius nature is so fine, so helpful to humanity, that persons of this Sign are necessarily found in every walk of life and every type of enterprise. In fact, it would be very hard for any great enterprise to get along without them.

Statisticians claim that a tremendous proportion of the world's most famous personages were born under this Sign, outnumbering each of the other Signs at a ratio of approximately 40 to 1. What makes it all the more pointed is that such fame has been judged in terms of humanitarian achievement, which is all the more credit to Aquarius.

THE EARLY PERIOD

Persons born early in Aquarius show selfish ways not common to this Sign. They have the humanitarian approach to life, but think of themselves first. This is due to the continuing influence of Sagittarius.

Belonging to Aquarius, these persons have many abilities, a depth of nature and a natural dignity, so it is more natural for them to concentrate on their personal development, rather than aim for an outside target. Thus they become subjective, with their minds on themselves, rather than objective.

This enables them to meet the disappointments that frequently plague Aquarius, but it increases their inborn gloom. They become aloof, exacting and sometimes almost stingy in their dealings, often creating a false impression of wealth and affluence.

Without knowing it, they may be cramping their natural Aquarius style. In contrast, we have:

THE LATE PERIOD

Here the Aquarius nature really spreads itself, but in an active way, due to the Jovian influence of Pisces. The late Aquarius period is so like the early Pisces, that it will be discussed in detail under that head.

♓

The Sign of
PISCES

PISCES: THE FISHES
(February 19–March 21)

FEBRUARY						
SUN	MON	TUE	WED	THU	FRI	SAT
1	2	3	4	5	6	7
8	9	10	11	12	13	14
15	16	17	18	19	20	21
22	23	24	25	26	27	28

MARCH						
SUN	MON	TUE	WED	THU	FRI	SAT
1	2	3	4	5	6	7
8	9	10	11	12	13	14
15	16	17	18	19	20	21
22	23	24	25	26	27	28
29	30	31				

Birth Stone:	Aquamarine or Bloodstone
Birth Flower:	Daffodil or Jonquil
Harmonious Colors:	Black, Green, Lavender, White
Ruling Planet:	Jupiter
Best Marriages:	Cancer, Virgo, Scorpio, Pisces
	Conflicting Sign: Libra

Here is the Sign of the Fishes, presenting art, skill and imagination all rolled into one. They are always active in a restless sort of way, much like the denizens of the deep themselves. Even when in seeming repose, they can snap out of it, fish-fashion, as though they had just been waiting to put their meditation into action.

The fact that they follow the tide does not mean that they are indolent or lacking ambition. Pisces persons are really "in the swim" more than any others. They will fight their way upstream when necessary, doing so much for the world as well as for people individually, that their efforts never will be forgotten.

On the contrary, the wise Pisces person is never foolish enough to battle the current when there is no need. This is not an individualistic Sign, but a social one. Those born under Pisces naturally crave companionship.

That goes for business as well as social life. Persons with this Sign need self-confidence. They can gain it from others if they choose the right associations. This they can do if they put their minds to it.

Being generous, they win friends. Having a receptive nature, they attract other people. But they must be smart enough not to let themselves be imposed upon. They must shy away from chance alliances, choosing only those which offer them a way to advance themselves.

Potential Greatness

Far from being selfish, that will be a great break for the other fellow. The reason is that a Pisces person seldom rates himself at anywhere near his full worth. So if he shoots way above his worth, he will come close to finding a proper partner or his right niche.

George Washington was a Pisces person. Whenever his army was defeated or disintegrated, he rallied the remnants and was in business again. When things fall apart, it is nice to have Pisces around to pick up the pieces. You are apt to find that you have more than when you started.

The Sign of Pisces is represented by two fishes, one up and one down. Which is headed the right way depends upon circumstances. That is for the Pisces person to find out. Meanwhile, in order to gain the success that he deserves, every Pisces person should develop whatever ability or talent he may possess.

Skill comes to Pisces naturally. Similarly, Pisces goes in for research and high art. They are good at handling detail and have good memories, particularly along specialized lines. In all, they have what others need.

So it behooves Pisces persons to supply those needs, to their own benefit. There, again, they will be benefiting others, which is harmonious to the Pisces nature. So the higher or more thorough the Pisces education, the better. To remain in ignorance can prove fatal to the Pisces nature.

Perfection vs. Procrastination

Pisces persons have an intellectual turn, but dislike any form of boastful argument. They meet things in a quiet way, so unless they have the knowledge to go with their convictions, they will be at a complete loss.

Given all that, Pisces is sure to win out. "Still waters run deep" goes the old saying and in those still waters, we find the Pisces personality as the sole owner and proprietor.

Pisces stands for Perfection and Procrastination. Those, you might say, are the names of the two fishes depicted with the Sign. Again, the question of which is which can be left to circumstances; but there is no doubt that one may work against the other.

In seeking Perfection, Pisces wants time. That is where Procrastination sets in. Asking too much of himself, the Pisces person may never get around to doing it. So it would be better to label those fishes: Purpose and Perseverance.

With Purpose as an immediate goal, Perseverance is naturally encouraged. It is possible to keep both in operation, even though they have to do with different interests. This will help enlarge the Pisces personality, adding still more to its development.

What to Avoid or Cultivate

As an example of the Pisces Sign:

When persons of this type acquire higher education, their unselfish nature encourages them to impart their learning to others. Thus they become great teachers, scientists or philosophers.

There the two fishes are symbolized, one swimming in one direction and representing learning; the other, headed opposite, indicative of teaching. Some of the finest Pisces persons have gone right through life operating on that "give and take" basis.

The Pisces nature must avoid despondent spells to which it is very susceptible. Flare-ups of anger, too, much be controlled. Even the finest Pisces nature "lets off steam" occasionally and when a Pisces person finds himself frustrated, he may ruin his future by too many of these uncontrollable fits.

VARIATIONS OF THE PISCES SIGN

Pisces persons, being susceptible to surroundings, show a craving for companionship, sometimes undulating as uncertainly as the watery element in which their symbolic fishes dwell, are naturally strongly influenced by planetary conditions.

It might be said that they absorb all such influences, accounting for many individual variations in the Pisces temperament. But at the same time, Pisces persons are greatly swayed by persons with whom they associate and sometimes reflect a borrowed personality as if mirrored in a limpid pool.

This soaking up of influences applies strongly to the adjacent Signs of the Zodiac, as in:

THE EARLY PERIOD

Here, Pisces absorbs the quality of Aquarius. They have the business sense of Aquarius, plus the Pisces sense of sufficiency, so they are able to get ahead of the game, yet help others in a generous way.

This is true, too, of those born late in Aquarius, who are closely related to those born early in the Sign of Pisces. The Jupiterian, or possibly Neptunian activity of Pisces becomes a volatile force indeed.

Leadership, skill, the desire to help others, are a threefold symbol as sharp as the prongs of Neptune's trident. But persons born late in Aquarius or early in Pisces, are not always able to make others see things their way.

Then these persons may become unfortunate and unhappy. Caught by a chance turn of the tide, they will hold to mistaken ideas and ideals, sacrificing everything while others profit. But, given full control, they show great executive capacity and can win out over vast adversity.

THE LATE PERIOD

When Pisces absorbs the upcoming Aries qualities, with all their Martian flare, the result is an urge for strong, effective action. This seldom reaches the fighting pitch, at least not visibly, for such persons use insight to accomplish all that combat could.

They also combine hindsight with foresight to an uncanny degree. Quiet, industrious, they plan a campaign as a chess player would, usually with brilliant success. Theirs are battles of the minds, but distinguished by an innate spirit of fair play.

This carries over the line into Aries, but there, the more aggressive nature of The Ram begins to gain sway.

PLANETARY SYMBOLS

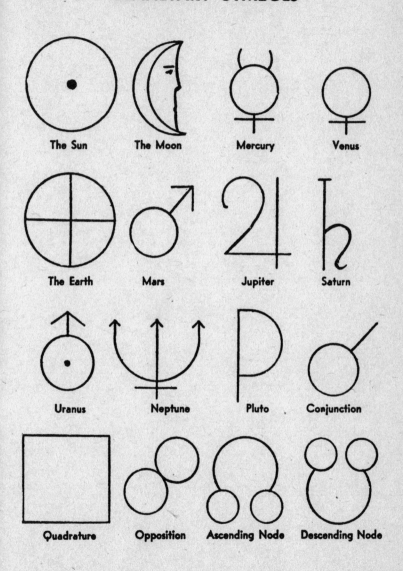

The Sun   The Moon   Mercury   Venus

The Earth   Mars   Jupiter   Saturn

Uranus   Neptune   Pluto   Conjunction

Quadrature   Opposition   Ascending Node   Descending Node

The Planets and Their Powers

Along with the twelve Signs of the Zodiac that gird the sky, the Ancient Astrologers listed seven Planets, or wandering orbs, as having a governing effect upon specific signs and mankind as well.

These Planets include the Sun, the Moon and five other members of the solar system; namely, the planets Mars, Mercury, Jupiter, Venus and Saturn. Actually, the Sun and Moon are not true planets, a term which in Astronomy is applied only to those bodies like the Earth, which revolve about the Sun; not to their satellites, or moons, of which the Earth has only one—the Moon—while some other planets have many.

But we are dealing here with Astrology, so the Planets must be considered according to their ancient status, but with a modern interpretation. Just as the Signs of the Zodiac have been likened to present-day road maps, the Planets may be regarded as the routes that can be marked on those maps.

Each Planet has a governing power over certain Signs of the Zodiac, as follows:

THE SUN governs the Sign of Leo.

THE MOON governs the Sign of Cancer.

MARS governs the Signs of Aries and Scorpio.

MERCURY governs the Signs of Gemini and Virgo.

JUPITER governs the Signs of Sagittarius and Pisces.

VENUS governs the Signs of Taurus and Libra.

SATURN governs the Signs of Capricorn and Aquarius.

Each of these Planets represents certain powers, qualities or limitations as applied to the individual. Just as you can speak of an Aries person or a Gemini person, you can refer to a Martian type or a Jupiterian nature.

But you must think of this as being superimposed upon the background represented by the Sign, just as a route would be marked. Thus, a Mercurian would find different outlets for his quick nature if he happened to be born under Gemini, than would another person of Mercurian qualities who might have Virgo as his Birth Sign.

The routes are not fixed and fast. Individuals can choose them for themselves. Thus a person born under Virgo would do well to apply his Mercurian quickness to things that conform to the Virgo nature. He should see that his Planetary powers are used to help his career, not to hinder it.

The same applies to all other Planets in relation to the Signs that they govern. As a result, the Planets, as related to the Signs, show just as many millions of chances for distinct individualism as do the Signs of the Zodiac themselves.

The individual should first study his Birth Sign; then the Planet that has power over it. From that, he can discover the active and passive phases of his nature, finding ways of self-expression and other potentials. He may also realize the need for controlling certain trends or impulses, aiming them more toward the fulfilment of his natural purposes and higher ambitions.

Planetary powers vary and they also intermingle. Thus, having studied the Planet governing a personal Birth Sign, the remaining Planets should be checked to find the periods in which they show a definite sway.

For instance, the Planet Mercury governs the Sign of Gemini (May 20 to June 21) but during the latter part of Gemini (June 12 to 21) The Sun is also a governing factor, as will be found under "The Sun" heading. Other examples will be found in the pages that follow.

The positions of the Planets at the exact time of a person's birth have an important bearing upon that individual's career. To go into this, it is necessary to draw up a special Horoscope, requiring comprehensive calculations. Rather than go into such exhaustive details, it is very possible to probe one's own personal inclinations and find out through self-analysis and logic just what powers may be at work.

This is not overly difficult, when handled in a broad way. Take the Gemini case given above, where the individual is definitely a Mercurian but showing a distinct reaction to the powerful influence of the Sun. These points are traceable and definable and can be checked off at the start.

Now, suppose that same person displays a highly sympathetic nature, involving a regard toward family and friends as well as all others who appeal to that individual's generosity. Obviously, this shows a touch of Venus. Without doubt, there must be some strong evidence of that Planet's presence where this person's inclinations are concerned.

You don't need a Horoscope to find it. But

the chances are that if you make an individual Horoscope in such a case, the position of Venus will be well marked at the time of that person's birth. So by studying the Planets and their powers, an insight and understanding may be gained regarding the ways and lives of many people who conform to such known indications to a highly marked degree.

The
SUN

The Ancients must have recognized the Sun's importance as the center of the Solar System. They not only gave it primary importance in the life of every individual; they regarded it as the chief of all the Planets, which significantly enough are under the Sun's control.

Physically, the Sun is the life center of humanity, as it provides the light and heat so necessary to existence. That very factor led to the worship of the Sun under various titles in many ancient lands.

From the standpoint of Astrology, the Sun's presence in a specific area of the heavens establishes the Sign under which an individual was born. That has already been stated in connection with the Signs of the Zodiac. But in addition, the Sun, like all the other Planets, is the dominating force over one specific Sign, that of Leo.

As the Ruling Planet of the Sign of Leo, the Sun imparts a fiery, resplendent power to all persons born under Leo, which as a result has gained itself the name of the "Royal Sign." This means that pride, love of power, in fact all kingly qualities are found in persons born under Leo.

Whether this is for good or bad, remains a question that depends greatly upon the reaction of individuals who have felt the Solar influence. It seems certain that a fulfilment of the Sun's majestic promise is a good enough guarantee of its powerful influence.

Disappointments are due, however, to those who fail to live up to the Sun's planetary promises, or who find themselves unable to do so. Unless they can achieve the full brilliance that brings due recognition, they will find themselves written off as arrogant, haughty, dominating, overbearing, or anything else that goes with a superiority complex, which is something that many people resent for the very good reason that they regard themselves as inferior.

The Sun's influence is not confined to Leo, the Sign that covers the period from July 22 through August 22. It carries on into the Sign of Virgo until August 30, so vitalizing some persons of that period, that they exhibit far more of the Sun's commanding nature than the Mercurian quickness that is more commonly found in Virgo.

Just as the Sun itself is lavish with its warmth and power, so persons governed by its overwhelming influence show the urge to have their power felt in a beneficial way. There is nothing small about these Sun folk, particularly those born under Leo, but they must not trust large things to small-minded subordinates incapable of grasping or promoting big ideas.

The "do-it-yourself" rule applies to Sun folk in a very big way and the magnetic, almost hypnotic quality of the Sun personality is brilliant, indeed, sometimes to a blinding extent. This is peculiarly true of the early Virgo period just defined, wherein the Mercurian quickness often links with the Sun's power to deliver flashes of genius and inspiration.

Another period said to be under the Sun's influence is the ten days of Gemini, June 12 to June 21. While not as marked as the carry-over into Virgo, this period of Sun force can show striking results indeed, perhaps too much so. In vitalizing the Mercurian nature also found in Gemini, the Sun's grandeur may be diverted to some small or even unworthy purpose through some crafty Mercurian mood.

People of latter Gemini or early Virgo should therefore harbor their finer sentiments, never letting them get clouded with mundane motives that will dull or ruin their Sun-given proclivities. They should choose high motives, adding sincerity to any natural warmth.

The Sun often strongly influences the middle belt of Aries (April 1-10) and middle Scorpio (November 2-11) adding fire and vigor to the Martian spirit which is at its height in the two periods mentioned. Here you will find an inexhaustible strength of purpose, but such people, like those of Leo, must guard against being wasteful in their ways.

They should use their influence to govern others wisely and justly, with control of self as an example. If they dislike taking orders, they should console themselves with what authority they do have, keeping confident that they will gain more.

Late Capricorn (January 11-20) is susceptible to the Sun's warming influence in a strengthening, beneficial way.

The
MOON

Much has been said regarding the Moon's influence on earthly existence. A book could be written on the subject. We know that the Moon causes tides in the ocean and that earthquakes have been attributed to its pulling power.

The Moon's effect has been studied on vegetation, in the flow of the sap in trees, the planting and harvesting of crops. From these, it is but a simple step to the study of the Moon's physical effects on human affairs.

These, in turn, may be linked with the mental. We know that many people undergo periodic changes, both physical and mental, which tradition has associated with the phases of the Moon. But Astrology is more subtle in its interpretation of the Lunar influence.

Astrology ascribes a Planetary function to the Moon, just as with the Sun. The Sun is the powerful, life-giving factor in wordly affairs; while the Moon governs the more subtle side of human nature, such as the senses, the desires, all the softer and more changeable moods of the individual personality.

The persons whose lives come most directly under the influence of the Moon are those born under the Sign of Cancer, or The Crab, as the Moon is the governing Planet of the period, which runs from June 21 through July 22.

It must be noted, however, that the Moon, through its own susceptibility, draws heavily upon attendant Planets, adding their influences to its own. This is very important, for Luna, unattended, would be a hopeless influence.

The Moon signifies sympathy, sensibility, home-loving traits, self-denial and other humane qualities, but these virtues are all of a negative or self-effacing sort. Their value can be wiped out by worry, hesitancy, indecision, change-ability and all the varied moods that fluctuate like the Moon itself.

However, with the support of other Planetary influences, these weaknesses can be mini-mized. Unless those other forces are given too much sway, the governing influence of the Moon will tend to bring out all their virtues.

Thus, we see the influence of Mercury is very strong in the first portion of the Crab Sign, persons born from June 21 on toward June 30 being quick, clever, versatile and so much on the go that they can snap out of the indecision so common to the Moon, showing practical sympathy and purposeful self-denial rather than mere maudlin sentiment.

Toward the end of the Crab Sign, from about July 15 onward, the exuberance of the Sun adds energy and brilliance to the Lunar nature. But there is always the danger that persons born in such periods will try to be what they are not. If they abandon their softer Lunar qualities, they will merely become weak sisters of the Twins or a very harmless Lion.

The Lunar influence may be felt in the belt of Taurus (May 1-10) adding a highly romantic touch to a powerfully emotional nature. Due to Venus, persons of this period are already loyal in love, fond of family and friends. You can note addition of the Lunar influence when they dote on June nights, seek romantic places or talk of second honeymoons.

Changeability manifests itself here, in the way they can switch from practical loyalty to sheer sentiment, practically feeling the joys or sorrows of loved ones, or going into ecstacy over old times and friendly reunions.

It has been claimed that the Late Virgo Period (Sept. 16-23) is under Lunar influence, but it is more likely that the vacillation shown by persons born at that time is due to the approach of the finely balanced Libra Sign.

Where the Moon does show a powerful effect is during the belt of Sagittarius (Dec. 1-10) where changeability of nature and choice of complex interests completely confuse the lives of persons born directly under that Sign. Such traits, when observed, are Lunarian and must be curbed.

When the late period of Aquarius (Feb. 10-Feb. 19) shows a changeable, uncertain nature, it too can be regarded as Lunarian. What persons confronted with this condition should do, is strive to cultivate their proper Planetary influences, which in this instance will be found under the head of Jupiter and Saturn, though other powers are at work, as will be seen.

It sums to this: In any horoscope where the Moon figures strongly, its influence will be highly evident and often unpredictable. Whenever other Planets balance or offset one another, the Lunar influence may also become an irresistible force.

The Planet
MARS

In modern times, Mars has loomed to prominence because it is the planet which can best be viewed from Earth, giving rise to theory that life either may exist there, or that the planet may at least be habitable.

But the astrologers of yore regarded Mars purely as an influence on human affairs and to Mars they attributed the aggressive and pugnacious qualities of the God of War, whose name the Planet bears.

Thus Mars is reputed to activate the Signs of the Zodiac which it governs; namely, Aries and Scorpio. This is appropriate enough, because both of those Signs show strong, aggressive qualities.

The Aries nature (March 21-April 19) is incessantly active and frequently combative, while Scorpio (Oct. 23-Nov. 21), when once aroused, becomes the most pugnacious Sign in the Zodiac. But Mars, in each instance, is more to blame than the Sign itself.

Those Signs are merely energized, even though it requires very little provocation for Mars to go into action. This is perhaps the quickest, most forceful of all the Panetary influences. Therefore, the rule is this:

If born under either Aries or Scorpio, it behooves the individual to restrain himself at all times and, most specifically, when roused to anger. Then, their Martian nature asserts itself too soon, giving away their intended moves, which often may be ill-advised.

There are other periods in which Mars shows itself as a definite governing force. One of these is in the late stage of Pisces, manifesting itself from March 12 on through March 21. Here, the Martian power is cumulative, gaining full sway with the arrival of Aries.

In fact, once the placid, deep-flowing Pisces nature is really stirred to action, Mars becomes dominant, supplanting the high-minded Jupiterian influence with Martian tactics.

Something of the Martian influence may carry into the Sign of Taurus, but only briefly. The Taurus nature, when stirred emotionally, becomes not only powerful, but often irresistible, but not through any yearning for conflict.

The Martian influence displays itself not so much through outbursts of mere rage, but in a hard, metallic manner, running from cool, calculating love of battle to ruthless tactics or outright cruelty.

Properly controlled, well-applied, it adds spirit where most needed. Often Mars becomes dominant in the mid-belt of Capricorn (Jan. 1-10) giving energy to that too-abiding and overly self-conscious nature.

Most Capricorn folk profit from such flares of Martian temperament. If action and anger stir them to too great measures, they usually find a way to make amends or revert to their more normal character.

Often, such persons have achieved surprising success through their Martian overtone, but there are times when their actions become unpredictable and therefore downright dangerous. They should learn the causes of any such flare-ups and take measures to curb them.

Even more serious is the Martian influence when found in the mid-belt of Gemini (June 1-June 10) where it takes on coldly vengeful characteristics that will stop at nothing, yet which are controlled in a cunning way.

The mythical Heavenly Twins, Castor and Pollux, were noted for their power in battle, and Ancient Astrologers must have noted that joy of combat reflected in the natures of those born under those two bright stars of Gemini.

If they have it, they show it in their eagerness to pitch into any controversy and establish themselves as champions of some cause. But they fight to win and accept a compromise only as a means to renew the fray along lines more to their liking.

Here, the crafty Gemini nature is at its best or worst—usually the latter. Their sharp, individualistic tactics can lead to rifts, even with their friends, for the Gemini fighter thrives on controversy and dissatisfaction.

Watch out for that Martian force in mid-Gemini! There is no telling the size of the tempest it can stir!

The Planet
MERCURY

The Planet Mercury

The tiny Planet Mercury scoots around the Sun in a mere 88 days, so that anyone dwelling on that world would live through more than four fast years in the time taken to experience just one full year on Earth.

Whether the Ancient Astrologers guessed at that, we do not know. But they were aware enough of Mercury's behavior to regard it as a quickening factor in the lives of all persons born under its influence. To Mercury, too, they ascribed a certain mystery, due to its comparatively brief appearances above the horizon.

In classifying all substances into the four elements of Air, Fire, Earth and Water, ancient savants were perplexed by one strange metal, which instead of being solid actually acted like liquid.

So they named it "mercury" as representing the Earthly substance most representative of the Planet Mercury, both in behavior and from the standpoint of mystery, there being nothing else resembling this "quicksilver" as it was later called.

In Astrology, we find Mercury as the governing influence over the Signs of Gemini (May 20-June 21) and Virgo (Aug. 22-Sept. 23). Both of these natures show the quickness and adaptability representative of the Mercurian sway.

With Gemini, Mercury acts upon the desire for change of companions as well as scene, the truly insatiable urge to go places and do things. With Virgo, Mercury has a similar effect upon the desire to find out new things, learn all there is to know about a subject and to switch from one project to another.

Whatever the physical factors involved, the action is chiefly mental. The Gemini nature can accomplish much in very little time when activated by Mercury, because the quicker the work is done, the more opportunity it finds for play.

Whereas, Mercury quickens the Virgo mentality to the point where it turns work into fun. Much of the Virgo activation is "all in the mind" with flights of fancy taking the place of the real life experience so essential to the enlivened Gemini personality.

Mercury will urge the Gemini person to go out to the race-track and play the horses, which they may do with surprising success due to their quick sizing of a situation. But that same planet will set Virgo's analytical mind to work figuring out systems to beat those same races.

This planetary influence turns Gemini folk into promoters and Virgo folk into producers. Given opportunities, both will snatch them when Mercury sways. The positive power of Mercury really goads both Signs into success,

Mercury can cause its human subjects to outwit themselves. It will start the Gemini mind on a merry-go-round, or harness the Virgo mentality to a tread-mill.

When opposition rises, the Mercurian nature tries to outrun it, as with Gemini; or to outshine it, as with Virgo. In either case, they expend far too much energy, wasting their cleverness and talent, only to see it all too late.

There are moods to Mercury, because that planet has its phases like the Moon. But they are due more to fluctuations in its influence. That is, the increase or lessening of Mercury's force will leave the individual following the more general inclinations of his own Sign, or cause him to feel the sway of other Planetary influences.

The Mercurian influence is often strong in the mid-belt of the Sign of Cancer (July 1-10) for the simple reasons that the Moon, which governs Cancer, is so susceptible to all other

Planets that it is quickened most by Mercury; plus the natural affinity of their phases.

This attunement of Mercury and Luna is mostly for the good, as it snaps the hopelessly uncertain Crab folk into much needed action. But Mercury, when it demands a change of clime or purpose, will brook no delay. It changes minds as well as moods, turning indecision into fret and fuming.

Don't expect Mercurians ever to explain why they did things wrongly. It's bad enough with Gemini and Virgo folk, with whom the influence is innate. But when the placid Lunarian, drifting with the Sign of the Crab, is quickened by Mercury into unprecedented action, he often winds up bewildered.

Mercury is regarded as influential early in Sagittarius (Nov. 22-Dec. 1) and in Mid Aquarius (Jan. 30-Feb. 9) but supposed Mercurian trends of these periods hinge largely on other Planetary influences.

24

The Planet
JUPITER

Ancient Astrology classed the mighty Planet Jupiter as the finest and most fortunate in the sky, long before Astronomy discovered that Jupiter was indeed the greatest member of the Solar System, the Sun of course being regarded as mightier in its own right.

Naturally, the Sun rates first, but being so highly influential in all the Signs of the Zodiac, much of its power is shared by all, with much of its energizing force being lost during the periods which it more specifically holds control.

But not so with Jupiter. Here Astrology really called the turn. In fact, Jupiter's influence may be regarded as that of a lesser Sun (which early Astronomers actually believed it to be) because it bestows some of its benign force upon every Sign of the Zodiac.

The reason why Jupiter is particularly powerful in the Signs which it specifically governs is because the favored mortals born beneath those constellations are able to absorb its grand enlightenment to the full. Their only weakness comes through disturbing influences that may also happen to prevail.

Those happy Signs are Sagittarius (Nov. 22-Dec. 21) and Pisces (Feb. 19-March 21) and

Jupiter endows persons born at those times with wisdom, optimism, and a personal magnetism that seems to sway other persons like the influence of the great Planet itself.

The term Jupiterian denotes "light bringer" according to ancient lore and is synonymous with the word Jovian. From the latter comes the expression "jovial" signifying a good mood and, by further extension, joyful.

So you can see why Jupiter brings gladness, even exuberance, to those who receive its fullest influence and, most specifically, is this true of the Sagittarius clan. Their Sign is the Bowman and, with Jupiter to guide their aim, they can, like Jove of old, turn their shafts into thunderbolts.

But they seldom go that far. Their urge is for independence; their aim, when properly directed, is so set for a personal goal that they bigheartedly extend best wishes for success to all the world as well.

The Jupiterian influence is often noticeable in early Gemini (May 20-29), warms the fading strength of Venus, and helps curb the shrewd, quick Mercurian influence which is coming into the ascendant.

People born at this time may be very acquisitive, sharp traders and close, quick bargainers, yet have strong emotional trends and go all out for charitable causes, as well as seeking high honors. It is easy to recognize the mingling of Planetary influences, with Jupiter striving to gain dominance over such shifting, volatile natures.

Jupiter's influence is an excellent counterbalance to the Sun's power in mid-Leo (Aug. 1-10) and whenever you see a person of grandiose, overbearing manner who can relax into a kindly, humorous mood while retaining some semblance of dignity, you have proof of the helpful Jupiterian trend in combination with the Sun.

Jupiter also proves a good influence when strongly present in the Late Libra period (Oct. 14-23) giving dignity and confidence to a wavering nature whose emotion is disturbed by a somewhat aggressive trend.

The strength of Jupiter is so great in Sagittarius that it carries right into early Capricorn (Dec. 21-30), activating that period with much of the purpose so common to the Bowman. It is the Jupiterian influence that draws the people of this period from their too-scholarly Saturnine moods. Here all joviality should be encouraged.

That brings us to Pisces, which has sometimes been classed as a Sign unto itself. The Jupiterian influence has such depth with persons of this Sign (Feb. 19-March 21), sometimes evidencing so much solemnity or straight-laced mannerisms, that it has become a modern vogue to attribute such traits to the influence of Neptune, not Jupiter.

This is at total variance with the ancient concept of Astrology, on which present-day findings still are based. The existence of the Planet Neptune was not recognized by the Ancients and even those who conjectured that such an outsider might exist, would never have ascribed powers to it.

It is purely a modern concept, not without its dash of whimsy, to name Neptune as the God of the Sea, the governing Planet of Pisces, the Sign of the Fishes. So far as mythology is concerned, Neptune was merely the deputy in charge of those watery regions, a Junior Jupiter, so to speak.

So that brings us back to the original concept of Jupiter as the governing Planet of Pisces, imparting all its high-minded, honorable traits to natures so deep-rooted that they value integrity above all else.

Rarely, perhaps, does the Jupiterian influence stir a Pisces person to the point where the world can appreciate the nobility of such a nature. Once revealed, it becomes a pattern that all could well follow.

The Planet
VENUS

Next to the Sun and Moon, the Planet Venus is the most brilliant sight in the sky, so outshining the rest of the heavens that it rates almost a category of its own.

So impressed were the Ancient Greeks that they mistook Venus for twin luminaries of equal magnitude: One, the Morning Star called Phosphorous; the other, the Evening Star, Hesperus.

Odd that Venus should have been classed as its own twin. For it does have a twin in the Solar System; namely, our own Earth. Modern Astronomers have learned the dimensions of Venus, have weighed it, in fact have done everything but go there, in order to come up with that finding.

The Ancients accepted this beautiful Planet as representative of love and therefore controlling the deeper and finer human emotions. They came to regard it as the governing Planet in the affairs of persons born under the Signs of Taurus (April 19-May 20) and Libra (Sept. 23-Oct. 23).

Persons with such birth dates show marked emotional tendencies but in strikingly different ways. Taurus is strong, filled with drive, but appreciative of fine things, with family and friends rating tops in that classification.

Venus literally provides the spark that turns the Taurus nature into a flaming torch where love and loyalty are concerned. This flares up all the more swiftly in the early Taurus period (April 19-28) because there the influence of Mars, itself a fiery Planet, has carried over from the preceding Sign of Aries.

This combination gives Taurus a Mercurian touch, for the rule, "All's fair in love or war" may produce a display of craft and guile that would shame the most scheming son of Mercury. But close study of cases will show that the early Taurus person confines those ways of cunning to the affairs of the heart alone.

You can count Mercury out, but that is all the more reason to beware the rivalry of the ardent suitor who belongs to this period. In late Taurus, Mercury does take hold, but in a way that lessens the Venus influence, sometimes even imposing upon friendship.

In Libra, the Venus influence is all love and sympathy, sometimes loading the scales until those factors are balanced against all else. These people will sacrifice everything for what they regard as a true, lasting love.

This is because Venus, like the Moon, has its phases. Viewed through a telescope at the time of its greatest brilliance, it shows only a portion of its surface, for it is then closer than the Sun and appears as a crescent. Only when most distant is the full form of Venus revealed.

Truly, without telescopes, the Ancient Astrologers must have sensed the flighty, elusive quality of Venus and named it accordingly. That Venus influence, working upon susceptible Libra, produces the very result to be expected— and more!

Venus sways Libra to a degree where the Planetary influence turns the social nature of the Sign into profitable channels, bringing fortune in business as well as in affairs of love.

Late in Libra, the Martian influence looms more and more into the picture, stirring persons of this Sign to the point where they will fight for love to hold it. This is because the Venus force lessens during the final week of Libra (Oct. 17-24) and such persons struggle to replenish it with Martian power.

Here, persons are fortunate if their Horoscope shows other planetary influence strongly affecting their individual Birth Date, because the Venus-Mars combination, although harmonious if well-balanced, can get badly out of hand, creating quarrels and misunderstandings.

Venus is highly influential as a growing factor during the late Aries period (April 10-19) warming the strong Martian nature of Aries and inspiring it to a sympathetic strain that may reveal touches of tenderness.

The affinity of Venus and the Moon, both having their changes and phases, gives Venus a sway in the early stages of the Crab Sign (June 21-30). This explains the remarkable understanding shown by persons of that period toward their family and friends. Though restless and changeable, they show a remarkable devotion and acceptance of responsibility that only the presence of Venus can explain.

Venus has an appreciable influence during mid-Virgo (Sept. 1-10) adding a sympathetic touch to the analytical ability so apparent in that period.

Also, Venus is helpful to the late Capricorn

period (Jan. 11-20) which greatly needs such influence to develop the artistry that is so real and yet latent in persons born at this time of the year.

♄

The Planet *SATURN*

Strangest of all the Planets is Saturn, a fact which was recognized by Ancient Astrologers, purely through their observations of its influence over mankind.

Odd, indeed that the Astronomers of a much later age should discover Saturn's curious rings which mark it as unique in the Solar System!

From time immemorial, Saturn has been the discouraging member of the stellar parade, even the word "saturnine" meaning morose and gloomy. But the fact is, persons born beneath Saturn's influence will invariably sink to the depths of despondency.

Not that they have due cause to do so. On the contrary, they represent some of the finest people in the world. But if you hesitate to accept the findings of Astrology, just put yourself in constant contact with the Saturn clan.

You will not only believe in stars, but you will thank yourself that you have lucky ones on your side! Even the run-around that Mercurian folk can give you will seem tame in comparison to the somber Saturn treatment.

Saturn isn't bad; it's good. It's not only good; it's the best. But it can become so exacting, piling up so many obstacles that must be conquered, that Saturn folk wonder somehow just where they are to begin.

Two Signs of the Zodiac come under the strong influence of Saturn. Those signs are Capricorn (Dec. 21-Jan. 20) and Aquarius (Jan. 20-Feb. 19). One follows right after the other, which means that Saturn delivers its deadly charge with both barrels.

The only difference lies in the reaction of the persons born under those somewhat contrasting Signs. The Capricorn folk accept their problems, then suddenly rebel against the whole idea. The Aquarius nature follows the do-gooder pattern, maybe dropping dead in their tracks while doing so.

In recent years, an Astrological *avant garde* has arisen, which has tried to shuffle off Saturn's sway over Aquarius by hanging it onto the Planet Uranus. Inasmuch as Uranus is scarcely visible to the naked eye and was never recognized by the Astrologers who for centuries established their findings in a highly convincing way, this can be written off as nonsense.

The fact that Saturn brings out almost wholly intellectual qualities of Capricorn persons, but develops what might be termed an inventive genius in Aquarius, simply shows how the underlying traits of those two Signs differ, plus the fact that Saturn itself has contrasting powers.

That, for our present consideration, is the most important point. It shows that Saturn is by no means baleful, but helpful. The only fault of Saturn is this: It stimulates the very urge that is already on its way to realization.

Capricorn has an intellectual urge which Saturn activates by providing more of that same intellectual factor, until the Capricorn nature just can't take any more of it. What is needed is some other influence to provide a varied development; without it, Capricorn goes despondent.

Saturn gives Aquarius false hope by stimulating the inventive features found there. But through them, Aquarius folk frequently go deeper into the rut, watching others profit from their ingenuity. This is natural enough, as Aquarius persons constantly try to help others and Saturn's influence does nothing toward showing them how to promote themselves.

Saturn influences other periods, too, and it is from those that we gain some clue from which

Capricorn and Aquarius can profit. For instance:

When Saturn influences the late portion of the Taurus Sign (May 10-20), it finds the Planet Venus already in sway. It's hard for Saturn to pull down the good-natured, beauty-loving Venus influence, which constantly seeks the lighter, brighter side of life.

All that happens is that persons born in this period experience brief spells of doubt and turn glum despite themselves, only to have their happier moods win out. Naturally, other Planetary influences may enter, from one source or another, giving Saturn too much sway. But all things being equal, Old Man Gloom (alias Saturn) will be banished.

Saturn can really take hold in the late Cancer period (July 13-22) which is already under the indecisive influence of the Moon. Here, melancholy can reach an extreme, unless the approaching influence of the Sun counteracts it.

Saturn often influences mid-Libra (Oct. 3-12) but there, the presence of Venus again has a brightening effect. In Libra, the constant desire to "balance up" is the danger. It may cause a person to give way to gloom after experiencing a run of pleasure.

The answer is: Don't let the Saturn influence carry the weight it does not deserve. With all its appeal to the intellect it is illogical. Laugh it off, let it run its course, or better still, harness it.

Improve the mind according to the Saturn way, then look for other influences to carry on.

Summary of
Planetary
Influences

After studying the tokens of each Planet and noting their varied relation to each other as well as to the Birth Signs, it is easy to see how widely the natures of individual persons may differ, even when their birth dates are close or identical.

From the standpoint of Astrology, the Planets are regarded as vital in the daily affairs of life and many persons constantly consult almanacs and other sources to gain up to the minute data on the subject.

Traditionally, each Planet is supposed to influence a given day of the week. Thus we have The Sun for Sunday, the Moon for Monday, Mars for Tuesday, Mercury for Wednesday, Jupiter for Thursday, Venus for Friday and Saturn for Saturday.

Two of these, The Sun's Day and the Moon's Day, conform almost precisely with English nomenclature. One, Saturn's Day, is taken directly from Latin.

In French, we find Mardi (Mar's Day) for Tuesday, Mercredi (Mercury's Day) for Wednesday, Jeudi (Jupiter's Day) for Thursday and Vendredi (Venus' Day) for Friday. The English versions come from the Norse equivalents of the Roman gods. As an example Thor is identified with Jupiter, thus Jupiter's Day became Thor's Day or Thursday.

Noted Persons
Born Under
Different Signs

Much can be learned about Birth Signs by studying the traits and careers of individuals born under them. This is a fascinating subject in itself and to encourage the reader to such research, examples are given of personalities born under different Signs.

Most of the Presidents of the United States have been listed as they offer an opportunity for close comparison. It is interesting to note the almost total absence of Gemini and Virgo from that group.

Other names have been chosen largely at random from exhaustive lists, the purpose being simply to offer those that are well-known or to give examples of occupations or talent that may serve as quick keys to natural traits.

NOTED PERSONS BORN UNDER ARIES

Hans Christian Andersen, Author of Children's Tales
Wallace Beery, Motion Picture Actor
Otto Von Bismarck, German Statesman
Charley Chaplin, Comedian and Pantomimist
Henry Clay, American Statesman
Thomas E. Dewey, Former Governor of New York
Washington Irving, Author of "Rip Van Winkle"
Thomas Jefferson, Third President of United States
J. Pierpont Morgan, Banker and Financier
Mary Pickford, Motion Picture Actress

Charles M. Schwab, Steel Magnate and Industrialist
Gloria Swanson, Motion Picture Actress
Spencer Tracy, Motion Picture Actor
John Tyler, Tenth President of United States
Frank W. Woolworth, Founder of Chain Store System

NOTED PERSONS BORN UNDER TAURUS

Louis Bonaparte, Napoleon III, French Emperor
Johannes Brahms, Master Musician and Composer
James Buchanan, Fifteenth President of United States
Marie Corelli, Novelist of Victorian Era
Bing Crosby, Singing Star of Screen and TV
Chauncey M. Depew,
                   U. S. Senator and Railroad President
Henry Fonda, Motion Picture Actor
Sigmund Freud, Famed Founder of Psychoanalysis
Ulysses S. Grant,
        American General, and Eighteenth President of
                                          United States
Sir Thomas Lipton,
                 British Yachtsman and Tea Merchant
James Mason, Motion Picture Actor
James Monroe,
     Fifth President of the United States and
                        Author of "Monroe Doctrine"
Admiral Robert Peary, Discoverer of the North Pole
Tyrone Power, Motion Picture Actor
William Shakespeare, English Dramatist and Poet
William H. Seward,
        U. S. Secretary of State and Purchaser of Alaska
Sir Arthur Sullivan,
            Musical Composer of Gilbert & Sullivan Fame

213

Harry S. Truman,
Thirty-third President of the United States
Arthur Wellesley, Duke of Wellington,
British General, Victor of Battle of Waterloo

NOTED PERSONS BORN UNDER GEMINI

Jefferson Davis, President of Confederacy
Sir Arthur Conan Doyle, Author of "Sherlock Holmes"
Ralph Waldo Emerson, American Poet and Essayist
George V, King of England
Julia Ward Howe,
Author of "Battle Hymn of the Republic"
Al Jolson, Musical Comedy Star
Basil Rathbone,
Motion Picture Actor and Portrayer of
"Sherlock Holmes"
Maurice Raymond, Internationally famous Magician
Rosalind Russell, Star of Screen and Stage
Harriet Beecher Stowe, Author of "Uncle Tom's Cabin"
Victoria, Queen of England
Richard Wagner, Composer of German Operas
Walt Whitman, Poet and Philosopher
Brigham Young, American pioneer and Mormon Leader

NOTED PERSONS BORN UNDER CANCER

John Quincy Adams, Sixth President of United States
Phineas T. Barnum,
Great American Showman of Barnum & Bailey Fame
George M. Cohan, Actor and Song Writer
James Cagney, Motion Picture Actor

Calvin Coolidge, Thirtieth President of United States
George Eastman,
> Photographic Inventor and Philanthropist

Mary Baker Eddy, Founder of Christian Science
George W. Goethals, Builder of Panama Canal
Harry Kellar, Famous American Magician
John D. Rockefeller, Financier and Philanthropist
John Wanamaker, Department Store Founder
Ferdinand Von Zeppelin,
> Inventor and Builder of Dirigible Balloons

NOTED PERSONS BORN UNDER LEO

Ethel Barrymore, Distinguished Actress
David Belasco, Playwright and Producer
Napoleon Bonaparte, Emperor of The French
Alexandre Dumas,
> French Novelist, Author of "The Three Musketeers"

Alexandre Dumas, Fils,
> Son of Alexandre Dumas, Also a Famous Author

Marshall Field, Mid-West Merchant and Philanthropist
Henry Ford, Pioneer Automobile Manufacturer
William Gillette,
> American Actor, Portrayer of Sherlock Holmes

Benjamin Harrison,
> Twenty-third President of United States

Herbert Hoover, Thirty-first President of United States
Francis Scott Key, Author of "Star Spangled Banner"
Julia Marlowe, Modern Shakespearian Actress
Sir Walter Scott, Author of Waverly Novels
George Bernard Shaw, British Dramatist and Wit
Eva Tanguay, American Actress
Booth Tarkington, American Author

NOTED PERSONS BORN UNDER VIRGO

James Gordon Bennett, Publisher of New York Herald
James Fenimore Cooper, Early American Novelist
Theodore Dreiser, Modern American Novelist
Elizabeth I, Queen of England
Greta Garbo, Motion Picture Actress
Charles Dana Gibson, American Illustrator
Maxwell Grant, Mystery Fiction Writer
Bret Harte, Western Writer and Humorist
Marquis de Lafayette,
     Espouser of American Independence
Charles Laughton, Motion Picture Actor
Henry Mencken, Author, Editor and Critic
John J. Pershing.
    U. S. Commander-in-Chief, World War I
William Howard Taft,
    Twenty-seventh President of United States
Leo Tolstoy, Great Russian Novelist
Wilhelmina, Queen of the Netherlands

NOTED PERSONS BORN UNDER LIBRA

Chester A. Arthur,
    Twenty-first President of United States
Sarah Bernhardt, Famous French Actress
Edward Bok, Editor and Philanthropist
Dwight D. Eisenhower,
    Thirty-fourth President of United States
Mahatma Gandhi, Political Leader of India
Greer Garson, Motion Picture Actress
Paul Von Hindenburg, German General and Statesman
Rutherford B. Hayes,
    Nineteenth President of United States

Jenny Lind, Concert and Opera Singer
Franz Liszt, Hungarian Pianist and Composer
Horatio Nelson, British Naval Hero
Guiseppe Verdi, Italian Operatic Composer

NOTED PERSONS BORN UNDER SCORPIO

John Adams, Second President of United States
Edwin Booth, Great American Actor
Admiral Richard Byrd, Aviator and Polar Explorer
Madame Marie Curie, Discoverer of Radium
Eugene V. Debs, American Socialist Leader
James A. Garfield, Twentieth President of United States
Edmund Halley, British Astronomer
Warren G. Harding,
            Twenty-ninth President of United States
Joel McCrea, Motion Picture Actor
Ignace Jan Paderewski, Pianist and President of Poland
James K. Polk, Eleventh President of United States
Claude Raines, Motion Picture Actor
Will Rogers, Actor and Humorist
Theodore Roosevelt,
            Twenty-sixth President of United States
John Philip Sousa,
            Bandmaster and Composer of "Stars and
                              Stripes Forever"
Billy Sunday, Baseball Player and Evangelist
Robert Louis Stevenson, Author of "Treasure Island"

NOTED PERSONS BORN UNDER SAGITTARIUS

Louisa Alcott, Author of "Little Women"
Ludwig van Beethoven, German Composer
Thomas Carlyle, British Author and Historian

Andrew Carnegie, Industrialist and Philanthropist
George Custer,
                    American General, Famed for "Last Stand"
Fiorello La Guardia, Mayor of New York City
Boris Karloff, Motion Picture Actor
John Milton, Famous English Poet
Franklin Pierce, Fourteenth President of United States
Lillian Russell, Famous Actress
Frank Sinatra, Motion Picture Actor and Singer
Zachary Taylor, Twelfth President of United States
Mark Twain, Author and Humorist
Martin Van Buren, Eighth President of United States
David Warfield, Shakespearian Actor

NOTED PERSONS BORN UNDER CAPRICORN

Ray Bolger, Motion Picture Actor
Stephen Decatur, American Naval Hero
Admiral George Dewey, Hero of Manila Bay
Marlene Dietrich, Motion Picture Actress
Millard Fillmore, Thirteenth President of United States
Benjamin Franklin,
                    American Philosopher and Statesman
William Gladstone, English Prime Minister
Alexander Hamilton, American Statesman
John Hancock,
        First Signer of the Declaration of Independence
Andrew Johnson,
                    Seventeenth President of United States
Robert E. Lee, Famed Confederate General
George G. Meade,
                    Union General in Command at Battle of
                                                    Gettysburg

Sir Isaac Newton, Astronomer and Physicist
Edgar Allan Poe. Writer of Weird Tales
Mad Anthony Wayne,
>	Famous General of the American Revolution
Daniel Webster, American Orator and Statesman
Woodrow Wilson,
>	Twenty-eighth President of United States

NOTED PERSONS BORN UNDER AQUARIUS

With the four Presidents born under Aquarius, the names of nine Presidential Candidates have been included in the list, all born under the Same Sign. This stresses the point that Aquarius is a Sign of prominence and leadership.

Note, too, that some of the candidates named were engaged in the closest of campaigns. Burr actually tied Jefferson in the electoral vote. Bell and Breckenridge together piled up more popular votes than Lincoln, whom they ran against.

Tilden polled more popular votes than his opponent, Hayes, losing out by a single electoral vote. Hancock ran only 5,000 votes less than the winner, Garfield. Blaine, too, figured in a very close contest.

George Ade, Noted American Humorist
John Bell, U.S. Presidential Candidate
John Barrymore, Stage and Screen Star
James G. Blaine,
      American Statesman and Presidential Candidate
John C. Breckenridge,
   U.S. Presidential Candidate, later Vice President of
                      the Confederate States
Robert Burns, Scottish Poet
Aaron Burr,
     Presidential Candidate, later Vice President of
                        United States
Charles Darwin, Author and Scientist
Charles Dickens, Author and Novelist
Thomas Alva Edison, Inventor and Scientist
John C. Fremont,
      Explorer, Soldier and U.S. Presidential Candidate
Samuel Gompers, Noted Labor Leader
Horace Greeley,
     Famous Journalist and U.S. Presidential Candidate
Winfield S. Hancock,
     Noted Union General, later a U.S. Presidential
                        Candidate
William H. Harrison, Ninth President of United States
Rupert Hughes, American Author and Historian
Thomas "Stonewall" Jackson,
                Celebrated Confederate General
Abraham Lincoln, Sixteenth President of United States
Charles Lindbergh, Famous American Aviator
William McKinley,
          Twenty-fifth President of United States
Douglas MacArthur, American General of World War II
Hiram Maxim, Inventor of the Machine Gun
Dwight L. Moody, Noted Evangelist

Wolfgang Mozart, Austrian Musician and Composer
Franklin Delano Roosevelt,
Thirty-second President of United States
Franz Peter Schubert, Austrian Composer
Samuel J. Tilden,
American Statesman and U.S. Presidential
Candidate
Wilhelm II, Kaiser of Germany during World War I
Wendell Willkie, U.S. Presidential Candidate

NOTED PERSONS BORN UNDER PISCES

Alexander Graham Bell, Inventor of Telephone
William Jennings Bryan, American Statesman
Luther Burbank, American Naturalist
Enrico Caruso, Famed Opera Singer
Grover Cleveland,
Twenty-second President of United States
Colonel William F. Cody, Famed as "Buffalo Bill"
Jimmy Durante, Stage and Movie Comedian
Samuel Houston, First President of Texas
Victor Hugo, French Author and Novelist
Andrew Jackson, Seventh President of United States
Elsie Janis, Musical Comedy Star
Henry Wadsworth Longfellow, American Poet
James Madison, Fourth President of United States
Adolph Menjou, Motion Picture Actor
David Niven, Motion Picture Actor
Augustus Saint-Gaudens, Famous Modern Sculptor
Francois Voltaire, French Philosopher and Author
George Washington, First President of the United States

History of
Astrology

Celestial observation has been a primary function of civilization throughout the known history of man. The earliest records showing the phases of the moon were made on bone on animal tusks. Early architects and artisans in every part of the globe erected huge structures dedicated specifically to stargazing. Wherever these astrological and astronomical records exist, reference is made to correspondence between the celestial and terrestrial worlds. An active science emerged to study the effects in nature, cycles of weather, agriculture, civilizations, and the destiny of kings. Influences on healing the ill and preparation of precious metals were everyday tools of educated people in these early societies.

The practical application of astronomical information, using apparent positions of the sun, moon, and the planets against the background of the stars, is known as *astrology.* Meanings were derived from these symbolic omens and applied to the affairs of man and nature. The underlying concept of astrological thinking is that happenings in the celestial sphere are reflected in events on earth and in human activities.

All mythological deities are tied to this planetary lore. Thor, or Zeus, is Jupiter; Apollo is the sun; and fast-moving Mercury was known as

Hermes, messenger of the gods. Deified human form was a symbolic way of understanding their influence in daily life. The circle of animals that evolved into the present-day zodiac were created with the same purpose in mind. The astrological alphabet of planets and signs furnished the basic tools of study for this ancient science.

The ancients realized that life in the earth was tied to the eternal law of change—cycles of day and night, spring and winter, abundance and famine. This law is best reflected in the Biblical commentary from Ecclesiastes 3:1-8.

1. For everything there is a season, and a time for every matter under heaven; 2. A time to be born, and a time to die; a time to plant and a time to pluck up what is planted; 3. A time to kill, and a time to heal; 4. A time to weep and a time to laugh; a time to mourn and a time to dance; 5. A time to cast away stones, and a time to gather stones together; a time to embrace and a time to refrain from embracing; 6. A time to seek, and a time to lose; 7. A time to rend and a time to sew; a time to keep silence, and a time to speak; 8. A time to love, and a time to hate; a time for war and a time for peace.

Records of planetary motion, the sun, and the phases of the moon exist in every culture on earth. Bone, stone tablets, papyrus, and huge monoliths, such as Stonehenge and the Great Pyramid of Giza, were used to record these events. The grand gallery of the Giza pyramid utilized a reflecting pool at the bottom, similar to the pool of reflective mercury utilized by the Naval Observatory in Washington, D.C., to observe the passage of celestial bodies across the meridian.

The ancients as well as modern-day physicists study man's tie to the universe. Science states that the entire universe is composed of the same basic building blocks. We live in a celestial environment of planets, solar system, galaxy, the universe, etc. . . . A new celestial consciousness is emerging with the many discoveries of our space probes. Unacceptable concepts are being rapidly vindicated. Venus, at one time thought to be a twin planet of the earth, is now known to be a searing, cloud-covered inferno whose rotation is in reverse direction compared to that of the earth. The list goes on and on.

The basic questions that stimulate this climb beyond the atmosphere with rockets, radar probes, radio, infrared detectors, telescopes, spectographs, satellites, etc. . . . etc. brings cherished notions of astronomy, physics, archeology, philos-

ophy, and religion to the brink of breakthrough—
or disaster.

And yet, out of this chaos of modern thought,
stand the basic principles of astrology, surviving
the ravages of time as a ragged refugee of the ages.
As Carl Jung conjectured, astrology is a com-
posite reflection of the breadth of human development . . . part of the mysterious imagination of
the subconscious reflected in daily living. With
great stamina and vitality, it has challenged the
greatest thinkers as the longest-lived legend in
man's cultural development next to the legend of
Atlantis. The general notion that anyone interested in the subject of astrology is tainted with
lunacy and charlatanism is rapidly deteriorating
in the light of a variety of new discoveries result-
ing from modern-day research. The world of impossible possibilities is upon us.

A new concept of ourselves as extraterrestrials,
harbored in an electro-chemical "space suit" appropriate for life on planet earth, is rapidly emerging. Through the various centers of the endocrine
system within the body, cells seem to respond in
sympathy with the celestial environment. Even
the air we breathe is charged with positive and
negative ions in sympathy to the solar flare activity of the sun. Positive ions create discomfort-

ing, irritable responses and ground the individual. Negative ions in the atmosphere usually create a cheerful relaxed mood, a feeling of well-being. The cause of solar flares themselves seems to be related to the positions of the planets in relation to one another in the solar system. The vision of all life forms, including man, as being linked with the activity of the celestial environment is not a new one.

Historical Survey

The priests of old were not unlike the scientists of our own day. They were the intelligentsia of their age. They did not relate their secrets to the general class of people. Language using the terms of their craft separated them still further from those of the masses. Knowledge is power, an equation that has not changed with our own era. Huge libraries around the world—Alexandria, Peking, the Vatican in Rome—attest to the fact that vast information resources were effective tools for controlling of civilization. Religion, science, mathematics, music, medicine, and cosmology, were each a part of the vision of body, mind, and spirit in luminous synthesis.

All major cultures of the ancient worlds were tied by a common esoteric language in symbolic form. India, China, Persia, Chaldea, Egypt, the Mayans in South America, and Hopi Indians in North America all had extensive use of symbols, including numbers and glyphs to denote ruling influences in the experiences of individuals. Rituals involving the activities of the heavens and energy from the sun and stars were created to give meaning to the mysteries of life. These ancient systems pervade the religious holidays of every world culture, including the Christian ones.

The celebration of Christmas was moved to the date of the pagan Saturnalia, winter solstice date of December 21, to make it more acceptable to new converts. Easter always falls in accordance with a prescribed astronomical formula, that is, the first Sunday after the first full moon following the spring equinox, March 21. The number of examples linking signs of the zodiac and the twelve prophets and the twelve disciples is contained in the Judeo-Christian tradition. The list can go on and on.

According to Cicero, in his book on divination, Chaldeans and Babylonians had records of celestial motion (used for navigation by both land and sea), which encompassed 370,000 years of history. Much of these priceless data were either destroyed or stolen by the many invading hordes.

Even this information suffered still further in the fires that eliminated the great libraries of Alexandria and Peking. A good example of a still existent calendar of that ancient information is that of the Mayas, who recorded the motion of the planets to an exactness of six decimal places! This is a feat that can only be duplicated by modern computers.

The great pyramid of Giza, itself reputed to be a calendar of thousands of years recorded on the inner walls of the interior chambers, is one of the few remaining remnants of the ancient records. According to Peter Tompkins' research as reported in his book, *Secrets of the Great Pyramid,* the very shape and dimension of the pyramid is in exact proportion to those of the earth. The pyramid duplicates in its outer dimensions the distortion of the earth—flat at the poles and bulging at the center. The height is less than the width. To acquire such knowledge, to build a structure oriented to true north and south, whose corners are corrected oriented to the solstice points and the polar axis of the planet, would require 2200 years of celestial observation.

The Egyptians used the planets and references to fifth-magnitude stars, almost invisible to the unaided eye, to orient this edifice of stone. It is reflective of reasoning beyond much of our capability to duplicate. Performed systems of math, engineering, and astronomical science without an apparent source were used to create this forty-story structure covering the equivalent area of seven square city blocks. Two-and-one-quarter million stones, carefully cut and dressed, each weighing between 4,000 and 24,000 pounds, were used in an engineering feat impossible to duplicate with our most advanced technology. Located at the center of all land masses on the earth—the 30th parallel of latitude and longitude—it represents a geological survey comparable in accuracy only to that recently accomplished via modern satellite. Some have inferred that possibly a technology totally unfamiliar to us was involved here.

As mentioned previously, the ascending passageway of the grand gallery creates a meridian slot for observing the culmination of any celestial body within a twenty-four-hour period. It catches the exact moment that a planet or star passes across the local meridian, an imaginary line that runs north and south at the locale, intersecting the ecliptic or path of the planets and sun. This technique is paramount in developing any body of astronomical knowledge.

Measurements around the pyramid have also revealed the expertise of the Egyptians in recording celestial motion. According to David Davidson, author of *The Great Pyramid, Its Divine Message,* the pyramid measures 365.2242 cubits around its base from corner to corner. This number corresponds exactly to the *solar day* or time it takes the sun to move across the earth's equator through one year to again cross the earth's equator during the spring equinox (approximately March 21). With the advent of photography, it was discovered that the pyramid was not exactly square but slightly indented along the sides. By measuring these indentations back out to the corners around the entire circumference of the pyramid, Davidson discovered that this equalled 365.25636 cubits of Egyptian measure. This number corresponds to the sidereal day as compared to the solar day of the previous number. This increment of time is the time it takes a star to appear at the same spot in the sky at the same time of year. It is approximately twenty minutes longer than the solar day and plays a vital part in the precession of the signs every 2,160 years, which equals one age.

The period of time it takes the earth in its orbit to make its closest approach to the sun is known in astronomical terms as the anamolistic day. This figure also appears in the measurements around the great pyramid. The many correspondences to mathematical formulae, the *golden section*, and *pi* are too numerous to elaborate on here.

Much of what comes to us today as the ancient tradition of astrology is from the Persian and Egyptian sources. Even modern astronomers have used the Egyptian texts to locate other planets. Such was the case with Pluto, rediscovered February 18, 1930. According to the Egyptians there are three additional planets yet to be discovered in our solar system. The Hamburg School of Astrology claims to have discovered these additional bodies plus five other sources of energy in our solar system.

The builders of Stonehenge understood that, by using a series of stakes coupled with the large stones, precise measurements could be made of the rising and setting of celestial bodies. Solar and lunar eclipse points could be predicted as well as the seasonal occurrences of equinoxes, as well as the spring and winter solstice points. Each stone is placed at 30° intervals, or moon stations, which record the daily motion of the moon.

Though there are only a few of these ancient observatories remaining for our investigation, certain deductions can be made. Gerald S. Hawkins, in his book, *Stonehenge Decoded,* states: " . . . many facts, for example, the fifty-six year eclipse cycle, were not known to me and other astronomers but were discovered (or rather *re-*discovered) from this decoding of Stonehenge.

"There can be no doubt that Stonehenge was an observatory; the impartial mathematics of probability and the celestial sphere are on my side. In form, the monolith is an ingenious computing machine, but was it ever put to use? As a scientist I cannot say. But in my defense, a similar skepticism can be turned toward other probers of ancient humanity. Do we need to see lipmarks on a drinking cup, blood on a dagger, and sparks from a flint striking pyrites to convince us that these things were, indeed, used?"

Hawkins and his team, using a large computer as well as the Smithsonian Astrophysical Observatory, Harvard College Observatory, Boston University, and the sight of Stonehenge itself, showed that the builders of Stonehenge had a classic concept of astronomical observation that today is called 'astrophysics'!

Advanced study of cycles provided the timing factors for raising crops and conducting their activities in attunement with natural rhythms. The

High Tor at Glastonbury, which is supposedly the center of "King Arthur's Round Table," is generally translated with each Knight representing one of the twelve zodiac signs. Each of these twelve signs is carved out in a five-mile circle in the surrounding landscape.

The complicated ley system, described in A View Over Atlantis by John Michell, is apparently tied to many of the ancient centers all over the entire globe. The Mound of Ching, the Dragon Paths, and the Great Wall of China, the temples of India and Greece, and the Pyramids in Egypt and South America *are all linked* through the ancient astronomical study with astrological interpretations. Records of the study of the heavens comprising centuries of observation correspond historically whether one researches the Mayans, Incans, Egyptians, or Chinese!

There are many other ancient resources available to the modern researcher, even manuscripts of the early Christian church. The Vatican Library in Rome probably contains the most extensive references to astrology and lost knowledge of any information center in the world. The gathering of its resources is due in part to the many inquisitions conducted by the Dominican Order, themselves expert astronomers and astrologers. In order to have an influence over the masses, these early church fathers believed in keeping them ignorant. They did not want knowledge disseminated but felt it should be kept in the hands of the few—knowledge is power.

The architecture, glass work, and sculpture of the churches in Europe still reflect the Masonic secrets in symbolic form. An example is the Chartres cathedral and its incorporation of the twelve zodiac signs rendered in various forms throughout. The appearance of the four fixed signs on each side of the Christ figure in the stone of the entrance speaks words of wisdom. It also bespeaks of the high esteem in which astrology was held by these early Christian church-builders.

These sculptured symbols and their representations are here listed:

Symbol:	Angel	Lion	Bull	Eagle
New Testament:	Matthew	Mark	Luke	John
Old Testament:	Isaiah	Daniel	Jeremiah	Ezekiel
Fixed Signs:	Aquarius	Leo	Taurus	Scorpio
Elements:	Air	Fire	Earth	Water

The Pope's bathtub is said to have the twelve signs enscrolled on its sides. Whether this tub is tucked away in some storeroom or is in use, I can't say, but the bathtub has been mentioned by several writers.

The challenge of astrological concepts has vascillated back and forth throughout history, but it is also noted that most of the great minds throughout the ages seem to have taken some interest in the subject. St. Thomas Aquinas (1225?–1274), Dominican monk, had as one of his duties the job of overseeing astrological activities for the Church. Copernicus (1473–1543) re-established the sun as the center of the solar system. Nostradamus (1503–1566), noted astrologer and seer, made predictions known to be accurate today. Tyco Brahe (1546–1601), brass-nosed Danish astronomer/astrologer, was responsible for the first astronomical observatory in the western hemisphere. Johannes Kepler (1571–1630), student of Brahe, whose laws of planetary motion are references for modern science, did extensive work to create a new astrology. These are just a few of the list of luminaries of the past who studied and practiced astrology, the oldest science.

In 1666 A.D., astrology was officially banished from the Academy of Sciences in France and from the universities. Yet, many mental giants of later dates still undertook to learn astrology. The world renowned poet, Goethe (1749–1832), pursued the study of astrology. Citations such as this might go on and on and would include most of the great minds of history.

The investigation of natural phenomena fostered by Asistotle and now heralded by the twentieth century of skepticism, has come full circle. The dilemma facing modern man is that we have investigated to the point of disproving all that our science seemed to prove in the beginning. Jacques Bergier and Louis Pauwels in their book, *Morning of the Magicians,* comment that science, theology, and philosophy, all dissimilar disciplines in their approach, are rapidly converging to the point of merging as one science. Skepticism faces destruction by its own hand; division and arbitrary judgment have given way to a holistic vision of the universe.

Kepler most appropriately heralded the increased interest in astrological principles of our own age by stating . . . "a warning to certain physicists, theologians and philosophers, who while rightly rejecting the superstitions of the astrologers, ought not to throw out the baby with the bathwater. Because it should not seem incredible that from the stupidities and blasphemies of the astrologers, a new, healthy and useful learning may arise."

The first signs of these new sciences began with the cycles of plant growth and weather. Svante Arrhenius (1859–1927), Nobel Prize-winning chemist from Sweden, undertook the first statistical investigation of the influences of the moon on weather and living organisms. The study of the effect of sunspots on human life soon followed during the period 1920–1940, conducted in part by A. L. Tchijevsky and Drs. Faure and Sardou. The frequency of sudden illness occurring in rhythm with sunspot cycles led to research in 1941 by a Japanese investigator, Maki Takata, using human blood serum. With the publication of *The Season of Birth* by E. Huntington of Yale University, the principles of the ancient science of astrology again reappeared as a reputable subject of investigation. Out of the remnants of lore and lost knowledge, a new science is emerging. Research in one area is being spearheaded by Frank A. Brown, Professor of Biology at Northwestern University, Evanston, Illinois. For the last fifteen years, his studies of exogenous rhythms have shown conclusively that plants and animals respond directly or indirectly to the position of the sun and moon. A whole new field of astrobiology or bio-magnetics has been started. Brown's research began with his study of oysters.

He found that the oysters, taken from the Atlantic Ocean, continued to open and close their shells in sequence with the tides on the Atlantic seaboard, even though they had been taken inland to Evanston, Illinois, along the shores of Lake Michigan. The pattern continued for two weeks, stopped for twenty-four hours, and then resumed in sequence to the tides [sic] corresponding to the moon passing the local meridian at their New Evanston location.

Rats sealed in closed environments, with constant food, constant light, and constant temperature were found to be *more active when the moon was below the horizon than when above it*. This illustrates that rats seem to be more aware of the moon's cycles than humans are.

Other recent research in physiological rhythms and social stress has revealed that human beings, though unaware, are extremely sensitive to the moon, too. These scientific studies promise profound impact on our day-to-day living, especially if we heed these natural, cyclic fluctuations. Illness, response to medical treatment, learning abilities, and job performance are likely to be affected by these cycles. Timing, in all our affairs, is of utmost importance, and a crucial key to evolutionary survival. It is certainly time for man to heed the work of these investigators of biomagnetism. Scientists have so far failed to come up with the most important discovery of all, which is the exact mechanism used to interpret these geomagnetic signals. As Brown points out, this is not unusual, as science has yet to discover the mechanism with which we identify smells.

As Shakespeare said, "There is a tide in the affairs of men, which taken at the flood, leads on to fortune; omitted, all the voyage of their life, is bound in shallows and miseries. We must take the current when it serves, or lose our ventures. . . ." *Julius Caesar,* Act 3, Scene 3.

The introduction of statistics and computers has aided the validation of many of the ancient principles. We are basically aware of the cycle of night and day, which has been extended with the use of modern electricity. Spring and winter have been altered by air-conditioning and modern heating systems. Studies of these broader cycles, such as those being done by the Foundation for the Study of Cycles, will certainly make us more the masters of our fate. In rescuing some of the old truths from obscurity and utilizing them along with newer discoveries, we will be harnessing more of the life forces available to us for our planet.

The movement of the moon has defied the greatest mathematical minds in predicting with infinitestimal accuracy precisely its orbital position. Only with recent discoveries made by our lunar probes, have we been able to make these precise calculations, which were necessitated by our venture into space. We now understand more about the moon's movement around the earth than we do about its geomagnetic effect on life.

The most obvious effect of the moon on the earth is related to the tides. The tide effect is a result of gravitational pull on the earth's surface by the sun and the moon. The new moon and the full moon create the greatest tidal conditions. The tides occurring on the side of the earth closest to the moon are the highest; so, the lowest tides are experienced on the side of the earth away from the moon. But did you know that there is an equal rise and fall of the landmass during maximum tidal periods?

Perhaps this phenomenon has some influence related to the occurrences of earthquakes and volcanic eruptions. So much is not known, that astrological explanations are as valid as mere conjectures by theorists; at least, there are some data available to astrologers.

The variety of research—in medicine and physiology, meteorology and biomagnetism, heredity and child birth, crime, and economics—is pointing to a new dimension for the use of natural cycles for the future. Man, armed with computers, statistics, space probes, etc., has revealed that astrological principles are a valuable human tool. Bergier and Pauwels in their work, *Impossible Possibilities,* state that by 1984 . . . "more and more scientists will be seeking to prove the theory of synchronization postulated by Carl Jung and Nobel Prize winner Pauli. This theory, which gives the ancient concept of fate a scientific underpinning through the idea that every man can be the master of the destiny determined for him through genetic and social factors, will form the axis of completely new sciences combining cosmology, psychology, and mathematics. Young people will dream of becoming cosmic observers or destinologists. These professions will be very difficult, but they will form the hub, the most significant orientation of science." Obviously the basic foundation stones of such an occurrence have already been laid.

It is important to keep this entire concept in a context of exactly *what astrology is insofar as affecting our destiny is concerned. Forecasts made regarding the celestial environment must always be treated as weather reports. There is nothing that can dominate the will of man once* he chooses to use this great source of creative action. Environment, heredity, and celestial influence are the dominant structures of life on the earth. If we allow them to rule us, we subject our will to a material view with no recourse. *Should we decide that we wish to utilize these astrological tools at our disposal to enhance our own growth, then we truly partake of our inheritance as "children of the universe."* The analogy of the space prober, or the deep-sea diver, putting on special attire to explore an alien environment is not far removed because our mind and spirit clothe themselves in the veil of flesh, a "space" suit, for the exploration of this three-dimensional world.

*Astrology
and
Your
Career*

In this day of cybernetics and the disappearance of many of the old-line jobs, it is more than ever necessary to know how you fit in and what is your best approach for a gratifying career. Many feel animosity toward automation and with some justification, for until the world becomes totally automated, the transition period is going to cause doubt, confusion and suffering from lack of work. Many will find they have just nothing to do.

It is wise to learn these new skills. Get a good training in some phase of the newly automated world. To be a skilled worker, hard work is necessary, but the skills to be learned will be satisfying and profitable ones, nothing like the old routine, tedious labors.

The Sun Sign messages ahead are intended to help you find the right way to assure yourself of a job that is congenial and also fits in with the new world in the miraculous age of Aquarius.

Aries

You enjoy competition and so long as work is not monotonous you can enjoy it, too. You want to take on the big jobs, be supervisor. Before you can do that you have to learn the rudiments, may have to spend quite some time with training. You need to have command of all details of your field, for a supervisor, more than anyone else, must be knowledgeable of every small bit of detail included in a job. You must be able to organize things from the bottom to the top. You'll dote on the machine age, the push-button ease, but you must understand the machinery in every particular. Seek to work in a brand new field.

Taurus

Your determination to count in the world will lead you to adapt well and to learn what must be learned to cope with the new. Age will not stop you from fitting in with the world ever. Your ideal is to be complete and accurate. You know that you must be realistic and wherever your work is, you will accept the new as it replaces the old. Whether it's the "new math" or the machines used in language training now, you will master the processes necessary to have a meaningful career that fits in. You may well take a course in computer skills and win a high paying position due to your ability to be logical and exact.

Gemini

You can be a whiz in mastering skills of communication or transportation in this world which keeps very busy with both. It's part of your artistry to be able to learn quickly the demands of the day. You like to be stimulated in your career, so do choose one which keeps your mentality challenged. Ideally you like to have several careers going at once or at least to have a career plus a hobby that may pay off, such as decorating. Be cautious of moving around too much in your career search, for you might not even stay around to learn anything thoroughly if you allow impulses to rule you. Find work so that you may use words, for that is your basic need.

Cancer

Cancer is threatened with career trouble, for it is not so easy to adapt to the new, and you incline to look with a grim eye at change which others accept easily. Actually you should have a leading position, for your talents are entirely equal to it. You may do very well in work with food which now has many amazing opportunities in processing. You will work well with furnishings and equipment for home. There are schools springing up all over the country now to help with domestic services and goods, and it would be well for you to embark on a course in one of these. Motel management could be the thing and you'd adapt.

Leo

You have your eye on leadership from youth on but you might want it all handed to you. This is not because you are not industrious; it is just that your regal nature assumes things will be given to you. You feel people will sense your royalty and ability to manage and thus catapult you into a top position. Not likely to be so! Show your abilities to handle emergencies, whatever your work is. Always get along harmoniously with work associates, and do not display arrogance or an attitude of superiority to them. Keep in mind that those in authority want the best one for each job and that diplomacy with subordinates is a basic requirement for any top job.

Virgo

You see to it that you have good training and you know that starting with a detail at the bottom is necessary to make a good executive in the long run. Never let yourself get bogged down in a trivial position, though. You will make a marvelous instructor for use of modern machines, and can thrive on the details you must know about them. Get training so that you can set up the machines for their work as well as handle the work itself as it needs. You will always keep control, for your memory will retain work at the bottom of the ladder. Working with words or research, statistics and charts will please you. Fulfill yourself.

Libra

You want to follow a career that allows you to feel harmonious with many. You can be an excellent boss because you believe in treating all people well and yet have a mind of your own that will control situations. You will do well in personnel management, counselling, public relations. You may have artistry that would fit in well in a decorator shop of your own. You might become head of the advertising department for a large concern and might be window-dresser for a huge store that always keeps beautiful windows as ads. You need to have a bit more willingness to compete; you like too well to stay a bit aloof and need to lessen pride.

Scorpio

You will not work where any executive does not have your esteem. You like the situation to be one in which you can learn. When you feel you are no longer learning anything, you may change your job or take a business of your own. A partnership is fine for you, if you find the one you have respect for the one who will work along with you. You like to be creative in your work, to feel that you are benefitting the world or its people. You can innovate and lead but you are just as happy in quiet work behind the scenes where you may be directing without the public knowing it. You could be a TV cameraman or director of the performing arts.

Sagittarius

You're happier the more you feel you are working in the spirit of the day, so what is new attracts you. You will study assiduously to learn the new skills. You want to show expert efficiency, to have all angles of your work very clear in your mind and under your control. You would like a career in writing or teaching, editing or publishing. You are fortunate with Jupiter as your ruler, and you may go to a top job more quickly than others. You might create envy around yourself. Be particularly cautious not to offend your peers or subordinates. You must feel that you can make changes for progress for to you the world moves—daily!

Capricorn

You will work hard but you want it to count. Everything you do in your career must contribute to some future attainment of the top position. If possible you want your own business, to be able to organize and direct with no one to hinder you. You can be pleased working for the government or for a major firm, if you have a position of leadership. You need a little time to get used to the new and must be patient with these swiftly changing days, and also must keep learning each day. You can teach well, take charge of a large office, be an excellent minister if you will go along with the very young who are changing church practices today.

Aquarius

You are aspiring rather than ambitious. You want a leading role in ushering in the new age which should bring happiness and love for all. You must get in with a cause or work that will let you feel you are a vital person in the new world that you see coming when old ills are erased for good. You want to see everyone fitted into work perfectly so they will be happy with what they are doing. You want to see payment enough for all to live pleasantly. You may work with labor and accomplish great things. You may have several careers for you do not feel bound to stay with any where progress cannot be made and seen. You may accomplish much with art or invention to brighten the world.

Pisces

You start in any work rather nebulously, feel your way around in it. Some of the newer machinery may alarm you; on the other hand, you may achieve perfect mastery of machinery if you are attracted to it and you might become an important person in the creation of even newer machines. You may work best for the law, for medicine, perhaps as a medical technician. You will be happy where you are helping people as in welfare work or the peace corps. You collect much knowledge and know that it is to be passed on, so teaching may attract you whether in an academic or trade school. You could be very attached to work in a trade school for it would involve your sympathies.

Astrological
Guide to
Decorating

How often we have said: "What interesting living quarters. I enjoyed being there but I would never decorate in such a manner." The differences in personal taste are reflected in our homes and our preferences are usually guided by the stars. Astrology tells us that no two people are precisely alike because no two persons can be born at the same time at the same place. Even identical twins are minutes or seconds apart. The tendency to surround oneself with certain colors and styles will help you understand the homes which you visit and may help you select the type of decor best suited for the astrological you.

Aries

Natives of Aries, a fire sign, are pioneers rather than fashion-followers. They care little about their environment if it makes them happy. They prefer bold warm colors and often mix them with careless free abandon. Furniture and artifacts are often blunt and heavy. You should not be surprised to find iron candlesticks or brass andirons. Because of their driving force, Aries people readily open their homes for political rallies, campaigns, drives and, as host or hostess, unconsciously become the center of attraction.

Among the clan of famous Aries people are

Charlie Chaplin, Charlotte Bronte, Albert Einstein, Joan Crawford and Doris Day.

Taurus

Those born under the sign of Taurus are practical, basic and have a keen eye for the value of money. Their homes are not filled with frills but with things that last. The furniture is solid and meant to be handed down from generation to generation. They search for "bargains" but only good bargains which will endure. Being an earth sign, you can expect a garden and if not that, many house plants which are carefully tended and nurtured. Taureans are especially fond of heavy wood and, being collectors, their homes usually contain wooden bowls, chairs and pictures in wooden frames.

Renowned Taureans include the names of Lionel Barrymore, Celeste Holm, Barbra Streisand.

Gemini

Gemini, an air sign of the twins, tends to produce people who are alert, eager to travel and revolt against monotonous regularity. These characteristics evince themselves in their environment. They enjoy changing the position of their furniture, collect unusual things which usually have no particular central theme but are interesting or conversation pieces. Theirs is a tendency to discount money if the article fulfills a whim. It has been said that the Gemini personality may be a headache but it is seldom a bore. Their homes reflect this imagination, duplicity and broad interests in many things rather than a deep interest in one.

Outstanding Gemini names are Marilyn Monroe, Sir Lawrence Olivier, Louis Armstrong, John Wayne and President John F. Kennedy.

Cancer

Those born under the sign of the Crab, a water sign, are referred to as Cancerean or Moon Children. Of all the zodiac these people are usually the most home-living and protective of their family and its sanctity. They tend to be extremely romantic, which shows in their surroundings which are often filled with antiques, dainty laces and frilly curtains. Their choice of color falls into the pastels. The male Moon Child prefers elegance which is not splash and his den is likely filled with perhaps fencing swords and rare old books rather than a case displaying modern rifles and a desk covered with risque magazines.

Famous Moon Children include Anne Morrow Lindberg, Empress Josephine of France, Pearl Buck, Ann Landers and Gina Lollobrigida.

Leo

The fire sign of the Lion produces strong personalities. Natives of Leo will fight to the death for their homes and those they love but they are not sheltering as are the Moon Children. Their personalities are usually paternal or maternal, showy, and can be melodramatic. This shows in their choice of decor. They prefer furniture that is massive, opulent and regal. Warm colors, gold, red and orange attract them and gold, in addition to its intrinsic value, is their favorite metal, a contrast to Moon Children, who prefer placid silver. They usually entertain lavishly whether they can afford it or not because they want to make themselves happy by making others happy.

Those who are born under the sign of Leo are typified by Jacqueline Kennedy Onassis, Napoleon Bonaparte, Princess Margaret of England, Mata Hari and George Bernard Shaw.

Virgo

Those born under the sign of the Virgin, an earth sign, are neat, tidy, with a place for everything and everything in its place. Their homes reflect their ability to catalog and to buy only good things which are unbroken and without a flaw. In all likelihood tables will be carefully placed with an ashtray on each so guests will not drop ashes and coasters readily available to avoid marring the furniture. Virgonians decorate their homes in good but modulated taste, preferring blues, greys, sleek easy-to-clean fabrics rather than velvets or chiffon.

Greta Garbo, Ingrid Bergman, Verdi and Leonard Bernstein are on the list of notable Virgonians.

Libra

Natives of the air sign Libra, the Scales of Justice, are very aware of the needs of others in planning their home or environment. Tactful and peace-loving, they are deeply interested in the artistic side of life which is reflected in the way they live. Their homes are well-arranged, with a good balance between furniture and fixtures, the outdoors and the indoors. Librans enjoy people and often entertain in an informal, sincere way but they are deeply concerned about the comfort of others. Usually natives of Libra prefer cool colors, blue, mauve, purple or soft greys.

Famous Librans are: Grace Kelly and Helen Hayes.

Scorpio

Those born under the water sign of Scorpio have quick observance and curiosity. They know a good thing when they see it and often find treasures for a small sum at auctions. Their homes, which are important in their lives, reflect these interests. Very often they will carefully unwrap something they cherish just for you to see it but not for the eyes of everyone. The real secrets of the home of a native of Scorpio lie below the outward surface. They are avid do-it-yourselfers and they work painstakingly well. In all probability, since natives of Scorpio are researchers, you will find many books and dictionaries in their homes. By choice they usually prefer paisley prints, quiet but unusual patterned fabrics from which they find a hidden meaning.

The natives of Scorpio, known to most of us, are Voltaire, Mark Twain and Walt Disney.

Sagittarius

Those born under the fire sign of the archer reflect their interests in their homes which, if they have a choice, are rambling and have room for activities both of an intellectual and physical nature. Their environment likely includes books, maps, things they have collected on hikes or camping trips. The garage may be filled with hunting and fishing equipment. He or she is fond of people and pets but the Sagittarian places living things over and beyond neatness; comfort is more important than style. Their homes are usually a mixture of modes, patterns and eras. Purples, deep blues, woodsy browns and greens usually predominate the scheme.

Sagittarians include Sir Winston Churchill, Mary Martin and Frank Sinatra.

Capricorn

Those born in this 10th and earth sign of the zodiac are industrious and authoritative. Their environment is usually solid and stolid, featuring family heirlooms and, being time conscious, they usually have a clock of some kind in every room. The Capricorn, whose astrological symbol is the goat, tends to be active outside the home as well as in it. This drive often leads them to have a family room for committee work and community or church activities. In general they are happiest when surrounded by attractive but dark, somber hues.

Noted Capricorns include Benjamin Franklin, Joan of Arc, Charles Dickens and Charles Lindberg.

Aquarius

Those under the air sign of the waterbearer are independent thinkers, always ready to help others even if it means letting affairs of housekeeping run down. Being thoughtful people, they need a room for their own privacy and their own activities, which are usually many and varied. While they appreciate stately mansions of others, they choose more functional environments for themselves. Neatness is a means of better functioning rather than an end in itself. They are fond of electric blues and bright greens, solid colors to busy prints.

Aquarian names we all know include Abraham Lincoln, Jules Verne, George Washington, John Steinbeck, Eartha Kitt and Tallulah Bankhead.

Pisces

This water sign of two fish tied together tends to produce people who disregard fads or "tricky" things in their environment. However, their decor is often filled with exotic pieces of furniture or art work. They do not buy bargains just because they are cheap but are pleased when they find something they really need at a low price. They are happiest when they are by the sea or some other place of quiet. Apartment living is not their forte. Their choices of colors are usually muted and natural, with sea green being a favorite.

Famous Pisceans include Elizabeth Taylor, Vincent van Gogh and Casanova.

Astrology
& Diets

Why is it some people can engage in such delightful pastimes as eating lots of pastries and rich chocolates, while others have only to whiff these enchanting foods and literally seem to gain? This may not be fair, as many will agree, but it does seem to be the way the Stars decree it.

While doctors may point to metabolism, and explain in medical terminology why our enzymes do not convert our food into energy as fast as someone else's, and give us a diet to follow, it just isn't that easy to follow the diet. Many fall short of the goal our doctor has set for us, mostly because we are individuals, and we try to tailor the diets our doctor gives us to fit our individual appetites.

Astrology has some clues as to why we are different, one from another, and while it is not considered an authority, the science of it is being felt and respected more and more every day. There seems to be a cosmic plan, all relating us to sun-signs and the type of energy our sign has given us to burn. If a sign tends to retain water, or doesn't burn energy readily or easily, this sign would find it hard as a rule to lose weight, and very easy to gain. But if a sign burns energy quickly, that sign would be more apt to stay slim.

The cosmic plan for us is aimed at helping us

maintain good health, which of course includes staying slim and vital. If we use this cosmic plan wisely we have a tremendous power, all within our subconscious mind, ready to act automatically by giving us suggestions and commands designed to help us maintain a good physical and mental fitness.

To follow this path, it is wise to know and understand our sunsigns, our weaknesses and strengths, and to maintain harmonious thoughts around us as much as possible. Get rid of the negative and take on the positive, for we must first control our minds and emotions *if* we wish to slim or fatten, either one, for our minds control us. However, we should not try to be our own doctor and select our own diet, but should consult first with our own doctor for any health or diet problem we may have. Here are some hints for the sunsigns.

Aries

With your impulsive nature you burn a great deal of energy, and, as a rule, should not be overweight. Your diet should emphasize wholesome foods that nourish as well as satisfy. Keep away from liquor or tobacco and cut down on the coffee and tea. Avoid bolting your food and try to keep the digestive tract free of distress. Avoid heavy breakfasts—cut it down to 1 or 2 poached or soft-boiled eggs and fresh fruit. Keep lunch light with perhaps a fresh salad, and follow with a good protein meat dinner *minus* potatoes.

Taurus

You tend toward plumpness for you truly like to eat, especially all of the rich foods and sweets. It is easy for you to gain, hard to lose. Best way for you to lose would be to cut down on the portions of food you eat, and this way you can have your cake and eat it too. Don't eat between meals unless it might be an apple, peach, carrot or piece of celery. Try to eat a good breakfast with 1 or 2 poached or boiled eggs, and some fresh fruit, or you might once in a while have cornflakes with a nice scoop of vanilla ice cream. Lunch should be light with a fresh vegetable salad followed by a good protein dinner. You generally need exercise, as you are prone to sit a lot and the circulation can become sluggish.

Gemini

You have a nervous, busy temperament, and are rarely overweight. But if you want to lose weight, try cutting out all of your heavy starches, and when you have to nibble, try apples, carrots, celery and raisins. You should really find it easy to diet. However, the best way for you to lose is to

271

find yourself a new interest and voila! Food should become less important to you! You need sufficient rest and relaxation, for you can suffer exhaustion at times if you do not relax enough or get balanced meals. For breakfast, you might have an egg omelet or hard boiled egg, plus some wheat germ coated with honey and skim milk. Try a raw vegetable salad for lunch with some juices, and a good, nourishing protein evening meal.

Cancer

You are inclined to be emotional, sensitive, moody. You do love to prepare food and to eat it as well, but tend to retain water, as well as gain weight. Nervous stomach upsets can occur due to eating while upset. Avoid, too, emotional food binges. You should exercise better self-control; eat a good breakfast with eggs, fresh fruits. If your doctor agrees, go on a 2 or 3 day liquid diet to try to shrink the stomach. Let sweets and starches alone, and eat lots of fish or seafood, salads made with fresh vegetables, and fresh fruits. Swimming can be a good exercise, as well as tennis or golf, to gain control of stomach muscles.

Leo

You are rarely fat, for you burn energy too quickly for that. I do not believe you find it hard to diet, but rather that it is easy. Keep down the calories and get lots of protein, fresh vegetables and fruits. Get fresh air and sunshine, proper exercise. You love the gourmet type of foods and sweets, and you generally eat too fast. Try to slow this down and maintain a healthy well-balanced diet.

Virgo

You are usually health and diet conscious, so rarely are fat. But if you wish to lose, try to cut down the portions you eat and leave the table before you are full. Your nerves can make you frustrated at times and send you on a snack binge, sure to add the pounds. Instead of eating the wrong snack foods at these times, be prepared with snacks of celery, carrots, apples, peaches. Have a good breakfast with eggs and fruit, a light lunch of salads and fresh vegetables and a good protein dinner.

Libra

Due to your desire for pastries and sweets, it is very difficult for you to stick to a diet. You continually say, "Just one more" and always break training. Try reaching for a peach, apple or pear when you have an immense desire for a sweet. Or for breakfast have a melon, wheat germ with honey. For lunch a fancy, fresh vegetable salad could be a delight for you, and for dinner a good protein *meat* meal with fresh vegetables and fruit for dessert. Avoid at least an excess of starches and potatoes. You should drink plenty of water and juices. A balanced diet makes for better harmony within the body. Leave the calorie-laden sweets alone.

Scorpio

I believe you have all the willpower necessary to go on a diet; all you have to do is *decide* and you can do whatever you decide to do. Use lots of protein—chicken, turkey, fish, eggs, cottage cheese, and fresh vegetables. For dessert fresh fruit is great! You do love *rich* foods and can be quite a gourmet when it comes to preparing or dining on the finest foods. Fruits are necessary for you, and alcoholic beverages should be avoided.

Sagittarius

You are a fire sign with much energy and drive, yet you do love to eat, especially exotic foods and generally eat quite a lot. Once you decide to diet, though, you should have no trouble sticking with it. Your main problem generally stems from improper circulation, although you have strong recuperative powers. Best for you to decide to begin a new *food* program; learn to eat differently with less calories in the amounts you eat. Chicken, fish, turkey, eggs, cottage cheese, fresh vegetables and fresh fruit for dessert should assist you. Keep a calorie counter handy.

Capricorn

You do not generally generate much body heat, can be gloomy and depressed at times—all tending to send you on a food binge. Be more optimistic about your life, what you can do. You should organize your diet well, in a business-like manner. But try to maintain a good balanced diet with plenty of fresh vegetables and fresh fruits. Being earthy in nature you generally like a meat and potatoes diet, but should eat lighter, using skim milk, cottage cheese, eggs. Avoid depressive moods that can send you to the cookie jar or ice box!

Aquarius

Being of a nervous temperament, you tend to like to nibble a lot. Doubt if you can stop this. However, try nibbling on less calorie-filled foods. Try nibbling on carrots, apples, celery, raisins, peaches and pears. Leave off alcoholic drinks, fattening snacks, creamed foods or rich foods. Get out and be more active. You can gain weight easily so you should do your best to limit fattening foods of all kinds. Use more protein, fresh vegetables and fresh fruits. Try some soft boiled eggs for breakfast and fresh fruit. For lunch, fresh vegetable salad, and perhaps some cheese toast; and follow with a good protein meat dinner, leaving off creams, and potatoes. Fresh fruit for dessert.

Pisces

You do love to eat, and can indulge in a bit of emotional snacking. You are somewhat psychic and retain influences reaching you from others. For this reason, it may be difficult for you to stay on a diet. Try eating chicken, sea foods, fresh vegetables and fresh fruits. Omit all of the rich creams, gravies, sauces, candies, sweets and pastries. For dessert try some fresh fruits, even a banana once in awhile. You need protein foods for energy. You tend to retain water and can gain weight easily. Best for you to avoid tobacco and alcoholic beverages.